Amazing Caring Woman

Cecile A. Labar

A publication of

Eber & Wein Publishing
Pennsylvania

Amazing Caring Woman

Copyright © 2017 by Cecile A. Labar

All rights reserved under the International and Pan-American copyright conventions. No part of this book may be reproduced, stored in a retrieval system, or transmitted in any form, electronic, mechanical, or by other means, without written permission of the author.

Library of Congress
Cataloging in Publication Data

ISBN 978-1-60880-618-8

Proudly manufactured in the United States of America by

Eber & Wein Publishing

Pennsylvania

Contents

About the Author 1

Introduction 3

Characters 6

Stage Directions 10

Act One 11

Act Two 38

Glossary 69

Amazing Caring Woman
About the Author

Cecile Labar was born in Kingston Jamaica in 1956. The family migrated to London England, when she was nine years old. She studied at Croydon College for the Certificate of Qualification in Social Work,1983-1985. She was divorced in 1985 after a seven-year marriage. Cecile Labar worked as an Education Welfare Officer/Education Social Worker from 1986-1990. She studied at The Center of the Media Arts, Manhattan, New York in 1991, and obtained a Diploma in Broadcast Announcing division. She returned to London and soon became pregnant, she is the mother of a son; her first and only child. She was a member of the Writers' Guild of Great Britain and New Producers alliance; and had read a number of books on how to write books and screenplays. Her first motion picture was finished in 2000, and was titled Amazing Caring Girls, this was changed to Amazing Caring Woman, and has been adapted to a stage play. She has written poems, lyrics, treatments these are formats, and is working on another motion picture. Cecile Labar was baptized when her son was five months old; at a Baptist Church. She returned to New York, Long Island, with her son in 2001, and she became a Seventh-day Adventist in 2011. She has been working as a Shop Assistant, then has a Home Health Aide since 2005.

Introduction

These three young women, Misty Boaz, Teresa Kwame, and Elena Mayer became good close friends; due to the fact of living in the same area. They have known each other for five months.

Misty Boaz and Teresa Kwame, and their husbands are owner occupier of their town house, situated in Lee Park, London S.E.3. Elena Mayer, husband and son lives not too far away, in a large two bed-room flat.

Their social interactions enable the couple to have a friendship that is quick sighted, through understanding of their discernment, and influence is derived from intellect and respect, from which confident belief is found. Their houses and flat reflects, the social class of have and have not, in the era of 1998. Richness is tastefully highlighted through their social class, culture and social events. They are all British of immigrant parents. Whilst there is no obsession with their religious belief, they convey a precious value, of being under the direction of God and our Lord Jesus. Misty and Victor are both strong characters, with positive moral values about life; this also makes them outstanding friends, in a world where friendship is seen, for many as to what they can get out of it.

Misty Boaz, Teresa Kwame and Elena Mayer are happily married. Misty, Victor, Teresa and Fez are achievers, they have achieved their best, from and education system that have tried; to make provisions for pupils of West Indian and African families. These couples could tell you of socio-economic circumstances, prejudice, social discriminations and racism. How-ever these topics would not make good drama comedy. These couples are not vulgar, loud, or brash, they are gifted with a worldly intellectual wit. On a professional level, the young women are quite mature; however when they get together they sometime become school girlish.

Victor and Misty are catholic, with similar profession, and they are from the same cultural background. Misty how-ever have never been to St Vincent, her knowledge of the Island, comes from events being told to her by her parents; letters from their relatives in St Vincent, and books on the Island. Victor how-ever had spent two long holidays in St Vincent, he was taken to the Island as a boy of six years old; and after studying for his degree, he stayed there for two months. Victor come from a family of two siblings, his brother Michael lives in France, and his the second in command of an airplane. Victor has future plans to take Misty to St Vincent. He some-times speaks French and Spanish, languages he learnt at school. Misty comes from a family of three siblings, Cloud Levi and Sky Seth, Bauer Seth is Sky's husband. Victor and Misty met at Greenwich Antique Market, they were dressed in their Sunday best, Misty was looking at a plate, Victor was walking by saw her, and said to her, "I would not give him no more than £5.00 for it." Misty turn around and look at him, to this she replied "you're right."

Misty became the Senior Press Officer for the Royal National Theater, after the Senior Press Officer left and moved to Scotland. Misty had worked for four years as a Press Officer, before she applied for the job. Misty's experience and a successful interview, had awarded her the job as Senior Press Officer at a young age.

Amazing Caring Woman

The following lines are said in these languages:

Spoken in French.
Your hands are like silk down my back.
Tes mains me fait seutir come un velous sur mon dos.

Spoken in Nigerian.
Salam alai kun means peace upon you.
Alai kun salam means upon you peace.

Spoken in Spanish.
You're beautiful when you're angry.
Tu es bonita quando tu es entaldu.

The women share a bottle of wine, usually white because it contains fewer calories.

Characters

Victor Boaz

This character is a thirty-year old negro man. He has a strong positive personality, with a spiritual know how of what is right and wrong. How-ever he lives on his ego, this goes with his profession, as Editor of The Glitzey Magazine. He worries unduly about meeting dead-lines. He is sensitive to other people's comments and opinions, and is a support to them, and those who are less stable. He is a successful reliable employee, sound personality, well-balanced, and his steadiness and consistency applies to his marriage commitment.

Diplomacy is necessary for an Editor, stories need to be sought with agreement, other-wise there may be complaints of unwarranted infringement of privacy. The Editor makes sure references and names are correct. An Editor needs to balance the wish to serve the needs of truth, and the desire for compassion, against the risk of sensationalism, and the possibility of an unwarranted invasion of privacy. Working for The Glitzey Magazine, Victor gains the opportunity to communicate with numerous people in the media. The Glitzey features glossy photographs, of famous black people; with articles of their life. People such as Members of Parliament, Actors, Actresses, Sports Personalities, Television and Radio Personalities, Models, Fashion Designers, Authors, Artists, Poets and Caribbean Cuisine.

Victor is a handsome man, when not wearing a suit, he wears trendy attire, and he is clean-shaven. He enjoys the company of the Mayer and the Kwame.

Misty Boaz

This character is of a twenty-seven-year old negro woman. Her appreciation of beauty, and her certain amount of concealment of thought, is a good ingredient in a well-balanced personality. Her sensitivity and deeper understanding, makes her a good communicator. She is a valued friend, she has a snobbishness at times, and this leads her to be critical. Yet it hints at a character with a highly developed artistic taste, and a good listener.

Her ego is expressed in her profession, as a Senior Press Officer, at the Royal National Theatre. She feels under constant pressure to get things done. How-ever her goodness and virtue, makes her someone to be relied upon. The team at the Royal National Theatre consists of five people. There are three Theatre at the Royal National Theatre, two production could be on show at the same time, as well as repertoires. She arranges interview with television, radio, News Papers and magazines; having met the lead Actor, to find out avenue of the media, they would prefer to go on, to promote the theatre play. She then makes contact with various people in these media organizations. She also arranges for photographers and critic, for the press night. She had gained a great deal of experience for working with various personalities.

Misty is an beautiful young woman, with tasteful trendy attire, she is happily married to Victor. She understands French and Spanish, languages learnt at school.

From time to time in the company of Teresa and Elena, Misty drift into patois.

Fez Kwame

This character is of a twenty-nine-year old Caucasian man. He is a handsome man, with trendy attire and fez hat, some-times colourful-ones, that make him stand out in a crowd. He has a certain amount of optimism, and is particularly glad to get out of a rut. He has the resilience to get back to normal, after physical or emotional set back. He likes the unusual.

His parents are Caucasian African Muslim, they are darker of the Caucasian race. The family history of migration is from Senegal to Nigeria to Morocco. The family has relatives in Morocco.

He is the proprietor and manager of a highly technical business, thus allowing him personal recognition of bearing his name. He video tape and edit some contracts. He is happily married to Teresa, and enjoys the friendship of the Boaz and Mayer.

Teresa Kwame

This character is of a twenty-six-year old woman, she is mixed race. She is attractive with trendy attire, she has a sound personality, and she copes well with the ups and down of life.

She is a valued friend and colleague, where she is one of the managers of the Calabash Day Centre, for the Caribbean elderly pensioners. Teresa's parents come from the Caribbean Island of St Lucia, and her religious background is Christian. Teresa is happily married to Fez, and she enjoys the friendship of the Boaz and Mayer. She convers in patois, in the company of Misty and Elena.

Yank Mayer

This character is of a twenty-nine-year old negro man. Ralph Mayer, known as Yank is a skilled electrician, his attire for work are of the clothing wear by an electrician. He is a proud father to his son Gibrel and he is happily married to Elena. He lacks excitement and fire, and he takes second place to his wife, who is a more natural leader. He often leaves it to his wife to take the initiative. How-ever he is a man who can be relied upon. He has a tendency to be negative about other people's ideas; and reveals a slight pessimistic out-look on life. His accent is of a strong Jamaican patois. His confidence grows from the friendship with the Boaz and Kwame, and he becomes more assertive in his marriage. When socializing, he wears casual clothes. He comes from a Christian up bring, although he does not go to church.

Yank Mayer was taken to Jamaica by his mother, when he was one-year old, his grandmother took a liking to Yank, and suggested that Yank stayed with her, Yank's father was no longer in his life. His mother being a single parent stayed with Yank for a few years, and then returned to London, she got married and had two children. Yank returned to join his mother when he was fourteen years old; Yank has a good memory of the years spent in Jamaica.

Elena Mayer

This character is a twenty-six-year old negro woman. She is a young attractive woman, with attire that's in fashion at the time. She is a working mother, and manages to do both with help from her mother. She is a worrier for her family financial future, but this is kept in balance through her budgeting. She has a certain amount of optimism, she copes resolutely with the ups and down of life. She has the resilience to get back to normal after any emotional set back. Elena is a hair dresser, her business is a small rented space, in Deptford in door shopping. It's called NEW WAVE, it consists of one hair dresser wash basins, one hair dryer, one hair steamer, and work surface for two chairs. Her business although small, has been successful.

Elena is happily married to Yank, and she enjoys the company of her friends Misty and Teresa, and in their company, will converse in patois.

Gibrel Mayer

This character is of a three-year old negro boy. He is stimulated when playing with a new toy, and he likes to learn and explore the world around him. He makes others feel joyful, especially adults. He likes to play with other children, and he likes to mimic what he hears on the Radio, and sees on the television. He also sings nursery rhymes.

His parents and grandparents love him. The name Gibrel derives from the name Gabriel, he is an Angel, also man of God or God is strong.

Stage Directions

The stage divide into two, with a wall, one partition as a set, and the other as a set, the stage revolves for each act.
For the horse riding, a made-up horse head with a long stick is use.
The car is a made-up car, with stools for seats.
For the child, a realistic puppet child that can talk.
Left and right means, stage left and stage right.

ACT ONE

The curtain rises.

Misty, Teresa, and Elena are sitting in the living-room of Teresa's house. For their usual coffee morning. Misty is talking about a track, on the long-playing record, by Steve Wander.

    MISTY: I wouldn't want Victor to call me is morning cup of tea. For that matter, what brand of tea! Brook Bond PG Tips, Assam, Jasmine, Early Grey or Lady Grey. [Misty laugh at her cynicism, Teresa and Elena also laugh.]

    ELENA: [raise her eyebrows.] You know it's tasteful to be called your morning cup of tea. If you think about it, why! A cup of nice tea could be light, refreshing, aromatic, delicately scented, and it would be served in bed!

    TERESA: Mmmm since you put it like that, his lyrics is sort of flavourish! [they giggled. Teresa got up from her seat, and poured wine into their glasses..] [Frowning.]

    TERESA: The only romantic thing, that comes out of my Fez mouth, in his way of expressing tender words, is to call me 'sugar dumpling', and that's not original! [Teresa sat down into her seat. Misty and Elena took a sip from their glass.]

    MISTY: You're right, sugar dumpling isn't original, beside you're not shapeless.

    ELENA: What about being called, honey sweet?

    TERESA: I like it, although it's a typical American expression, honey!

    ELENA: A friend once told me, her husband called her 'sweet potato'! [They giggled and took a sip of wine. Misty laughing gasp for breath.]

    MISTY: Aaaa, such terms of endearment. Do you know the word 'alcorza' means a kind of sweet meat.

ELENA: No. You mean something like 'sweetbread'!

MISTY: No it's meat cook in something sweet, like in a barbeque sauce.

ELENA: Oh. [They took a sip of wine.]

TERESA: The first part of the song conveys privacy, admiration, and about settling down and making a home. It's definitely alluding to proposal of marriage. Tell me Elena how did Yank proposed to you?

ELENA: Him put him hand on mi stomach, mi lowered it to mi lower abdomen, ye mi said to him, we are expecting! With excitement in his eyes, as though turned on with attraction! He popped the question! [Teresa and Misty laugh. Teresa poured more wine into their glass.]

MISTY: I see you had your work cut out for you, he didn't know where the developing embryo was!

ELENA: A so it goes! You right to call it embryo! You have no idea how relieved mi was then. [Elena took a sip from her glass, and put the glass down on the table next to her.]

ELENA: Mi had no money to support a baby then, what mi get as shop assistant; paid mi rent, paid mi bus fare, fed mi, and kept mi clothed.

TERESA: Yank is a good man... Many would run from their responsibility.

MISTY: Yes, you're right, he's a good man, and Gibrel looks just like him.

ELENA: Uno two can tell mi about your proposal later, let's get back to the song. [Elena had a chuckle in her voice, she wanted to change the subject, feeling acute anxiousness, for being brought back to a time of ambivalence. Teresa and Misty sense Elena anxiety, were willing to do as she asked.]

ELENA: Remember the bit, about a lifetime fantasy of being with the only one, who can create his paradise!

MISTY: I see what you mean, a lifetime fantasy, definitely gives the impression of knowing each other since childhood.

TERESA: Yeah do you remember your first boy-friend!

ELENA: Oooo yes! He was the kid next door, let me think now... mi was about four years old, and he was about the same age.

our parents would let us play together, in each other house and garden. Up and down the garden we went, on our three-wheeler bicycles…. You know he would kiss me, and I would kiss him right back, in front of our parents.

MISTY: What was his name?

ELENA: Oooh, aaa, I remember now, Matthew… You know our parents never said much then, not until mi teenage years, when they started with them rules and sanctions.

MISTY: My parents were the same.

TERESA: Mine too. [With excitement in her voice.] My first kiss was from a boy name Errol, we were living on top of mi parent's grocery shop. Good friends of mi parents would visit on Sunday afternoon, with their three children. They would stay all afternoon to early evening. Have dinner with us. Their two older children, would take us to the park. There we would play hide and seek. When-ever Errol found me, he would kiss me. I think mi was about four too, he was approaching five.

MISTY: Aaaa… I read somewhere that a frown, use up over forty face muscles. Just think, to poke yu lip, must use up about sixty face muscles. [They giggled, picked up their wine glass from the table, and took a sip of wine.]

MISTY: My first boy-friend was at the nursery. I tell you plenty of kissing went on there. We use to play dressing up. You know, Doctor and Nurses, mums and dads. Well, there was a little boy name Ron, who would make sure when it comes to kissing girls, I would be the one to kiss and set next too. [Misty paused for a moment, thinking.] How innocent we were as children, yet the mocking by primary peer group only bring back the feeling of sadness and rejection. For what seemed funny one minute seemed terrible the next. It's funny though, when the boys and girls would say yack, kissing! He would stop. I guess kissing in early childhood years seemed funny or forbidden… Although we were not aware of it, we were reinforcing healthy behaviour of bonding, influence by adult's behaviour of gratification and pleasure seeking energy.

TERESA: Is that Freud or Jung's theory?

MISTY: Freud.

ELENA: You mean like creating his paradise! Like on the record.

MISTY: More like his euphoria.

TERESA: No dear his ecstasy. [They took a sip of wine, Misty put down her glass and pick up a magazine, she turned the pages and put it down again.]

TERESA: The Glitzey is only sold monthly as you know.

MISTY: Mmmm.

ELENA: I like to read di magazine, it's the best.

[Teresa gets up from her set, and walk to the stereo record player; she lifts up the cover, the record was on the turntable, she looked for the track on the sleeve, and press down the switch, select the button, adjust the sound to a level of back ground music. She then lifted up the amplifier, and put it in between the groove of the track to be played. As Teresa was about to sit down, Misty raise her eyebrows, and in a sarcastic tone.]

MISTY: There is a bit in the lyrics, about there's a time when playing ends, and the serious begins like the love he felt from the start… With each beat of his heart. It's so good he sings it a whole heap of time! [There is a short moment of silence as they listen to the music, these moments shared together are greatly treasured. They began talking when the lyrics in the song, begins with there's a time when playing ends and the serious begins.]

TERESA: I see what you mean! He's going to put up with her playing around.

ELENA: No dear… Whatever she a do him a do! [They giggled and sipped on their wine.]

MISTY: The man lack values… A trust to mistrust. [They giggled.

TERESA: No dear. He's been around experienced a lot of failed relationship. He's going to love her, even though his heart would break!

ELENA: A winter in Eden but a summer in his heart!

MISTY: It's a willing victim of a crime, you can't blame love!

ELENA: No dear, a who knows what tomorrow brings!

TERESA: The flesh weak!

ELENA: The road is long, but they going to climb the stairs any way! [they giggle.]

MISTY: Seriously now, the lyrics is of the love he prayed for, before he goes to sleep. It gives us the notion of someone having religious credence. You see love grows, true love is bliss, and God desires for Godly couples is Godly and Heavenly…. If he has certitude, God Angles would help them; from making rush decisions. You know, from leading them into satanish or devilish behavior. Any-way, what we are saying is a conjecture, some virtues of human decency suggest, mmm, let me think… If a child lives with criticism, he learns to condemn. If a child lives with hostility, he learns to fight. If a child lives with ridicules, he learns to be shy. If a child lives with shame, he learns to feel guilty. If a child lives with tolerance, he learns to be patient. If a child lives with encouragement, he learns to have confidence. If a child lives with praise, he learns appreciation. If a child lives with fairness, he learns justice. If a child lives with approval, he learns to like himself. If a child lives with acceptance and friendship, he learns to find love in the world. [Teresa get up and walk to the record player, and stop the music.] [Elena sighed.]

ELENA: From our first kiss as children, we had learnt friendship, and as we grew-up we know how to love as adults!

TERESA: All what you just said is so true… Would you both like some of mi beef patties?

ELENA: [Spoke spontaneously.] Yes.

MISTY: [Spoke spontaneously] Yes.

TERESA: [Teresa got up out of her seat and walk, Right.] Help your selves to more wine.

ELENA: Horse ridding was great last week wasn't it? [Elena poured more wine into both their glasses.]

MISTY: Yes it was.

ELENA: Tell mi Misty was your bottom aching too?

MISTY: [Misty stood up and rubbed her bottom and inner thigh.] Yes! Mi bottom and inner thigh was aching fi days. [They laugh and Misty sat down.]

ELENA: How did you find the ridding stable?

MISTY: I was having driving lessons some years back; around the area of West Wickham, because my driving test was going to be taken there. I saw two horses and riders coming out the lane. I asked the driving instructor, if he knew where the horse ridding stables was. He replied "no", but he thought it would be good practice, to drive down the country lane, and that's how I found the stables. [Misty hearing the ratting of cups, got up and walk to the door and open it. Teresa enter the room with a tray of plates, cups, saucers, tea spoons, coffee pot, milk jug, sugar bowl, a plate pilled up with small beef patties and serviettes. They both return to their seats. Right]

ELENA: We were talking about horse ridding.

TERESA: It was great fun. [Teresa handed them a plate with serviettes.] Help your selves to some patties. [Teresa began to pour coffee into the cups, they help them-selves to milk and sugar.]

ELENA: It's now mi feel like telling yu, the biggest lie mi told Yank... Well you know what some black men are like, mi told him mi was pregnant! Hoping he would ask mi to marry him. When he did and wi started planning di wedding, it was then mi took every step to get pregnant.

TERESA: What would you have done, if you didn't get pregnant? [Teresa took a bite from her patty.]

MISTY: Yes! Some women take a long time to get pregnant. [Misty takes a bite from her patty.]

ELENA: Well, mi suppose mi would have told him mi had a miscarriage, and wi would have to keep trying. [Eating her patty.] Mmmm, these are nice.

MISTY: Yes they are.

TERESA: What about yu Doctor, Nurse, hospital, and all those kind a thing? [Elena sighed.]

ELENA: It's neither here or there now... The main thing for mi was Yank wanted to marry mi. Fi wi wedding day was extravagant! Considering wi didn't have a lot of money. Both fi wi parents had helped us, and with the joy of our son.... You know he never twigged, when Gibrel was a month over dew! [Teresa put down her plate on the table, and picked up her coffee cup and began drinking.]

Misty: What a relief that was for you, every-thing worked out well in the end.

TERESA: It's amazing! How did it work out with grandparents?

ELENA: Mi told the same speel bout Gibrel being over dew. [Drinks some of her coffee.]

TERESA: [With excitement in her voice.] Lets' get back to horse ridding. When Lorraine's horse went into a trot, I was right behind her, and fi mi horse started trotting too! Well it nearly took mi breath away! It was fun though.

ELENA: Lorraine said if wi keep booking lessons, in no time wi would be cantering.

TERESA: That would be a laugh!

ELENA: Yu think wi could do it?

MISTY: I'm sure we could, those horses are well trained.

TERESA: Who did you rode last time?

MISTY: [Giggling.] Mi rode Brandy.

ELENA: [Giggling.] Mi rode Whisky.

TERESA: [Giggling.] Mi rode Vodka. Funny names they give those horses?

ELENA: Yes! They're bizarre, as Misty would say. [Misty laugh.]

ELENA: Yu would have thought, names like ruby, freckles, and light-foot would be more appropriate for horses.

TERESA: Mmm.

MISTY: They use to use horse hair, to make wigs and hair extension.

ELENA: Before synthetic hair and human hair became fashionable.

MISTY: [Putting her fingers through her hair.] I have to search high and low to find the right, hair extension to match my hair and skin shade.

ELENA: Fi wi hair grows about two millimeters a week.

TERESA: Yu think it have any-thing to do with the melanin in our skin?

ELENA: No.. There's so much variation in the black race; its' because wi have tightly curled hair.

MISTY: Victor told me that the Caribbean Islands a mixed population of mixed race people. Of Indian and black, white and black, and Chinese and black.

ELENA: Yank said the same about Jamaica.

TERESA: We only have to look at the West Indian people in this country, to see how mixed up we are... It's a good job the local Government recognize, the need for a day center for the elderly black pensioners. If yu see some of them light skin ones, when yu hear them speak, a nothing but patois a come out of them mouth.

17

ELENA: Mi have an idea! Lets' take our husband out with us.

MISTY: It's a great idea!

ELENA: Lets' go to the cocktail bar and restaurant in Crystal Palace. Remember, [They giggled at the ambiguity of the cocktails.] Teresa had the slow comfortable screw, I had the screaming orgasm, and Misty had between the sheets.

TERESA: Why not! I'll make a reservation and phone you both in a few days.

[RIGHT. The **Manager** was standing by the front entrance of the restaurant.]

TERESA: You have a reservation for Misses Kwame?

MANAGER: Aaaa Yes, would you like to eat now or would you like a drink at the bar?

[Teresa look at the others, as though asking them what they want to do.]

FEZ: Lets' have a drink first. [Elena Yank and Misty nod.]

VICTOR: Fine with me. [The couples walk across the stage, the lights is focus on the couples at the bar. The rest of the restaurant lights is dimmed. The people at the tables were eating and talking, however their conversation, was not loud enough to be heard. The couples are given the cocktail list by the **Bar Waiter**. LEFT.]

BAR WAITER: When you are ready let me know. [The Bar Waiter made himself busy behind the bar, the women hardly look at the cocktail list.]

MISTY: I going to have a blue lagoon.

TERESA: A calvados for me.

ELENA: Mi will try the classic.

[Victor addressing his question to the men.]

VICTOR: Seen this one between the sheets!

FEZ: What about slow comfortable screw!

YANK: Yu no see the screaming orgasm!

[The women adapted a modest look, they are quite surprised at the coincidence of their husbands' mentioning the same cocktails they had drank.]

VICTOR: The three rivers look interesting.

FEZ: So does James Bond.

YANK: Fi mi is a whisky with ice.

[The **Bar Waiter** over hearing them reiterate their order, he had already started making their drinks.]

BAR WAITER: Did I here you ladies ask for a blue lagoon, a calvados, and a classic?

ELENA: Yes!

BAR WAITER: And for you gentlemen, was that a whisky with ice, a James Bond, and the three rivers.

VICTOR: Yes!

MISTY: Yank, tell me how did you get your name?

YANK: Well Misty, when mi did a breast feed as a baby, mi Mother said, mi was pulling hard on her breast, mi Father remark was, 'him a yank yu', and the name got stuck to mi.

[They laugh.]

YANK: Mi real name is Ralph.

MISTY: What about you Fez?

FEZ: My parents had visited relatives in Morocco. They had pin point my conception to Fes, a place they had visited, so they honored me with the name. It's odd though, it's spelt with a z. In fact my family history of migration goes back a long way. They migrated from Senegal to Nigeria to Morocco, we were racially mixed along the way.

[The Bar Waiter started to put their drinks on the bar.] [Has Fez was finishing his sentence, a woman came behind Misty and tapped her on the shoulder. Misty turned around to see who had touch her. She is surprise to see her Sister. Misty gives her a hug and a kiss on her cheeks.

SKY: Surprise to see you here!

MISTY: This is my older Sister Sky! These are my friends Elena, Teresa, and their husband Fez and Yank, and of course you know Victor. [Sky shake their hands, she walk over to Victor and kiss him on his cheeks.]

SKY: How are you?

VICTOR: Fine Sky how are you?

SKY: I'm fine too. I don't want to interrupt your evening out, so I going to go back and join my friend. [As she was walking away.] Oh yes, we are planning a barbeque, would you like to come?

VICTOR: We would love to.

SKY: Your friends may come along too.

[The Bar Waiter put the other drinks on the bar.]

MISTY: Where are you setting? [Sky point to the back of the restaurant by the wall, where a woman was sitting eating her dinner and looking at them. Sky took a step and turned around.]

SKY: Oh yes Cloud is coming too!

MISTY: I will phone you.

[Misty and Elena picked up their drinks and began to drink. Fez picks' up Teresa drink and handed it to her.]

FEZ: Here you are sugar dumpling. [Teresa took her drink and look some-what embarrassed, at being called sugar dumpling in a public place.]

YANK: Now Misty mi think a fi yu turn to tell us how fi uno di get yu name?

[Misty look at Victor, she was thinking of how many times she had told people, how they got their names. Victor knowing what Misty was going to ask him.]

VICTOR: No darling you tell them.

FEZ: You must have got some stick at school?

MISTY: Mmmm, the kids would say Misty, ask Cloud if it's going to rain! And Misty ask Sky if the Sun is going to come out! [They began to laugh except Misty and Victor. Fez took their drinks from the bar and handed them to Yank and Victor.

VICTOR: Thanks. [He began to drink.]

YANK: Thank yu. [He began to drink]

MISTY: Seriously now, my parents are Catholics and their reasons for giving us our names are, God Almighty created Heaven and Earth, and we their children are God's creation. So they bless us with these names. [Teresa look at Fez.]

TERESA: Your parents should have called you Morocco Mole!

YANK: Then yu must be Secret Squirrel!

TERESA: Well, he's always wearing them Fes hats!

VICTOR: They suit him.

YANK: Him look good.

MISTY: I think Teresa object, to you calling her sugar dumpling in public. [Elena laugh.]

YANK: A where yu get them phrase from?

FEZ: We were listening to some music one night. Teresa was taping them to play it to the old folks.

ELENA: Teresa is one of the Managers for the Calabash Day Centre.

FEZ: I though the song was amusing. [Fez began to sing a verse of the song.] Hay fatty boom boom, sweet sugar dumpling, not because you so big and fat, don't believe I'm afraid of that, self praise is no recommendation, I'm looking for creation. Hey fatty boom boom, I may look like a mouse, but I want bread, I won't stop till I drop down dead. Never let you big size fool you, cool as it is it may fool you, hey fatty boom boom... I sort of kept calling her sugar dumpling all evening, between many kisses, well like you Yank the name got stuck. [The waitress came over to them and approach Yank.]

WAITRESS: Would you like to be seated at your table now? [Yank whisper to her.]

YANK: Do wi have to?

WAITRESS: No!

YANK: Wi will finish fi wi drinks ya thanks. [Yank felt please with himself for his assertion. The waitress went away and attend to her duties.]

ELENA: [They alternatively look in the direction, of Elena's gaze and then face each other.] Look at di man sitting over there, don't look to make it obvious, see how him ears big, and one even look bigger than the other!

VICTOR: It's a scientific fact that one side of our body, is bigger than the other, but in his case it's stretching it a bit!

ELENA: Them remind mi of horse ears! Since wi have been going horse ridding, mi have become interested in animal rights, mainly those that are cruelly treated.

YANK: Di only horse mi ever rid was in the school gym!

FEZ: Me too!

VICTOR: Well I have to say, my horse ridding days was at school. I went to Saint Dunstan's college, one our school holidays involved horse ridding. I seem to remember falling off a few times!

MISTY: I had horse ridden before, during a school holiday exchange, with a school in Texas.

YANK: Texas U.S.A?

MISTY: Yes.

TERESA: Lucky you! I never went ridding until we went.

ELENA: Same here, but mi was concerned about their cruel treatment.

VICTOR: I see! Many animals are killed until they are extinct. In fact the international Whaling Commission, are lifting the existing moratorium on commercial whaling, and giving the Whalers an official quota.

FEZ: It would put Whalers out of work, given an official quota would help matters.

ELENA: Mi think Whaling should not be allowed.

YANK: A because yu no eat whale, if yu di eat them like di people in Japan; yu wouldn't think nothing bout it. Mmmm by the way the food smell good?

MISTY: Mmm yes! It is written, we have dominance over animals, but with all these scientific experiment going on today, it's becoming bizarre! Take for instance genetically grown crops!

VICTOR: Yes, it's frightening to think what the Government are allowing scientist to do! The world is not short of land to grow crops, farmers have been growing crops for centuries! Poor countries are short of money.

YANK: Them a clone sheep too!

FEZ: They got to draw the line some where! I would not like to think I would be eating some-thing that Allah did not create.

TERESA: What they expect us to do now, buy such food in the supermarkets!

MISTY: I hope not, in fact some animals are very useful, what would the blind do with out a dog!

ELENA: How true, it's us humans that are cruel.

[Victor look around and beckon to one of the Waitress.]

YANK: Talking bout cruelty Victor, being an Editor yu must know wa a going on wi the Serbs in Kosova?

[The Waitress came over to them.]

WAITRESS: Would you like me to show you your seat now?

VICTOR: Yes thanks.

[The couples put down their drinks on the bar, and follow the Waitress to their table. Fez went to the wash room to wash his hands. LEFT. The couples are seated in an half circle table, Yank and Elena to the left Victor and Misty in the middle, and Teresa and Fez to the right. The Waitress gave the women the menu, and the men the wine list and menu, Fez wine list and menu is left at his place at the table.]

VICTOR: Shall I order Chardonnay Misty?

MISTY: Yes please. Where did Fez go?

TERESA: He's gone to the wash room to wash his hands.

YANK: A wa wi have ya! Cabernet Sauvignon, La piat D'or, Soave, Valpolicella, Merlot, Claret, Elena how bout a Chardonnay?

ELENA: Yes Yank I think you have chosen well.

[Fez return to the table, sat down and pick up the wine list, the Waitress came back to the table.]

WAITRESS: Are you ready to order?

VICTOR: Yes.

YANK: Mi is no wine consir!

VICTOR: I think you mean connoisseur.

MISTY: May I have the salmon supreme.

ELENA: Mi too.

TERESA: Make that three.

VICTOR: Sirloin steak with mustard aioli, and a bottle of Chardonnay.

FEZ: Same here, and a bottle of Don Pavral.

YANK: Braised lamb shank, rosemary jus and mash, and a bottle of Chardonnay.

WAITRESS: How would you like your steak?

VICTOR: Medium well.

FEZ: Same here.

[The Waitress took their menus and wine lists, and walk away. They began to eat their bread rolls. LEFT.]

MISTY: Victor and I baby sat for Gibrel one Saturday, he was glued to cartoon network all afternoon. [Misty and Victor went into an uncontrollable laughter.]

VICTOR: Cow and chicken!

MISTY: Pork butts!

[They all started laughing.]

TERESA: I'm laughing but I don't know what the joke is about!

FEZ: Nor do I!

MISTY: Cow and chicken are cartoon characters, the cow and chicken parents are humans; they serve them pork butts for dinner, it's the round bottom of the pig with its' wriggly tail on a plate. I think what's funny is the pranks they get up to.

TERESA: We must baby sit Gibrel too.

ELENA: Your offer is accepted.
[The Waitress brought them the bottle of wines, she pour wine in the men glasses, then the women.. Yank was the first to try his wine.]
YANK: Mi no eat pork.
ELENA: Wi don't eat pork.
YANK: This wine could do with a little sweetness!
ELENA: It's ok.
MISTY: Chardonnay is a dry crisp wine.
YANK: Mi did have a good Rasta friend, when mi was a boy in Jamaica, he didn't eat pork, and he tell mi all bout Ja. Mi granny did think mi stupid fi a listen, to any think a Rasta man tell mi bout Ja.
TERESA: Fez is a Muslim therefore we don't eat pork neither, I use to until I met him.
FEZ: I'm considered to be a bad Muslim because I drink.
VICTOR: Misty and I studied the Laws of the Bible and Haftorah, we are thinking of giving up pork. But Fez you don't have to worry about the hereafter, I could show you many examples in the Bible, where it's acceptable to drink, you are safe with God if you drink with moderation.
MISTY: That's such a neighbourly thing to say Victor.
VICTOR: Our neighbours does not mean merely, one of the Church or Faith to which we belong. It has no reference to race, or class distinction, our neighbour is every individual who needs help, our neighbour is every soul who is wounded or bruised by the adversary. The Lord knows that no one could obey the Laws, in his or her own strength, only by accepting the virtues and grace of the Lord, can we keep the Laws.
ELENA: Also belief in the forgiveness of sin, help us to love God with our whole heart.
[Sky and Hilda came over to their table.]
SKY: We are leaving now, this is my friend Hilda, Hilda this is my sister Misty and her husband Victor, and their friends.
HILDA: Hello.
MISTY: Nice to meet you.
VICTOR: Hello.
[The others look and smile.]

HILDA: Bye.

MISTY: Bye.

[Sky and Hilda walk away and went out the restaurant. Right.]

TERESA: What does your sister live?

MISTY: Dulwich near the village.

ELENA: What does Sky do for a living?

MISTY: She is a Doctor, her husband is a Doctor too.

FEZ: Victor I hope you will think seriously, about writing a column on my business?

VICTOR: When the Feature Editor is less busy, he's so successful at getting proprietors interested.

FEZ: Bye the way Yank, I'm going to need your help, with regard to some electrical repairs in the shop?

YANK: Sure any time.

TERESA: I'm going to book an appointment next week, to get my hair wash and set, make sure you fit me in because, I'm not going to wait an hour just to get my hair done.

ELENA: Just tell mi the day and time yu coming and, I will mak sure yu get yu hair done.

[The Waitress came to their table with women's meal on a tray, and put it in front of them.]

WAITRESS: Salmon supreme, Salmon supreme, Salmon supreme, enjoy your meal.

MISTY: Thank you.

VICTOR: Please bring us three more bottle of wine, two Don Pavral and one Chardonnay.

WAITRESS: Will do. [The Waitress walk away. LEFT.]

ELENA: Remember when we all went to the Tate Gallery, Well I don't suppose you notice Yank showing Gibrel all the naked statue, and saying, "Gibrel my son this a yu first sex education lesson. Yu see him Charlie and the Chocolate Factory, now yu have one of them don't yu."

[The Waitress return with the men's meal on a tray, and put it in front of them.]

WAITRESS: Sirloin steak, Sirloin steak, and Braised lamb shank.

VICTOR: Thank You.

WAITRESS: It's my pleasure. [She walk away. LEFT.]

VICTOR: [Before they start eating, they bow their heads.] Heavenly father we thank you for friendship and the food that sustain us, and for those that prepare the food, in Jesus name Amen.
[Yank feeling so relax in their company, forgot any social skills he had, and pick up the lamb shank with his hands, and began eating. Misty look at Yank with shocked expression, her lower lip drop open. Victor notice the situation, felt embarrass, he tried to smooth the situation.]

VICTOR: I don't know Misty, remember when we eat those large prawn with our hands.
[The look he gave her remind her of the sexy feeling of that evening, she blush and smile.]

MISTY: Darling this is a restaurant, and we are not eating prawns.
[Yank look up realizing what he did, licked his fingers, then pick up his serviette and wipe his hands, then his knife and fork and continue eating.]

ELENA: Him no surprise mi a so him eat at home.

FEZ: Why I was brought up to eat with my hands, we eat dishes like ground rice, cuscus, and chey-bon-jen.

ELENA: Aaaa, that's why yu wash your hands!

TERESA: I have tried some African dishes; they are quite nice, my parents cook similar dishes. I make sure salt goes into the ground rice though.

ELENA: What's chey-bon-jen?

TERESA: It's Senegal national dish, it's rice, fish, vegetables in pimiento and tomato sauce.
[They look at Yank with wet mouths, and lick their lips as he describe, the delicious sweet ripe juicy fruits. The Waitress return with the wine, and put them on the table, and walk away. LEFT.]

YANK: When mi a boy in Jamaica, mi use to pick di ripe fruits in mi granny back yard, mangoes, guavas, custard apples, sweet cups, june plums, and star apples. Mi would give them a wipe in mi clothes, then bite into them. A tell yu the fruits them did perfume ripe, sweet smelling, and as mi bite into them, di juice just run down mi mouth.

FEZ: How did you reach them being a small boy?

YANK: When mi never climb di tree, mi use mi granny long stick, it had a hook at di end.

TERESA: I've not been to the Caribbean.

FEZ: I've not even been to Senegal or Nigeria, let alone the Caribbean.

ELENA: Mi no go di yet.

MISTY: Nor have I.

VICTOR: I went to Saint Vincent for two months, after my degree, but that's nine years ago.

MISTY: Knife and forks were not used, in this country until sixteen eleven, when Thomas Coryat returned from travelling France and Italy. He wrote about the Italians using a little fork instrument, when cutting their meat.

VICTOR: Why the earliest tool used for food, was a crude lump of fissile stone, called a flint. It was used to cut into things, as well as to make fire.

MISTY: Yes! In the early seventeenth century knife and two prong forks, were finely engraved with Biblical motto. Such as 'Love is the Foundation', and 'Put your trust in God'. Forks of silver and gold were used, by King Charles the fifth, and King Charles the sixth of France. However, they were only used for eating mulberries and foods likely to stain the hands.

TERESA: How do you know so much, about the history of knife and forks.

MISTY: I read it in an exhibition in the foyer at work.

[Victor stood up and pick up the bottle of wines, and top up their glasses.]

VICTOR: Please rise your glasses, here is to a caring, enriching friendship, maturity in the increasing knowledge of our God and Lord. Respect for our maturity of thoughts and feelings and, for the boundaries of our individual uniqueness, most of all respect shown for our own spiritual marriages.

[They all held their glasses and drank. Misty is now tipsy.]

MISTY: Praise the Lord, how lovely Victor, Victor was circumcise.

YANK: It's a nice speech, what's circumcise?

FEZ: Yes it was, I will tell you later.

[Elena and Teresa nod.]

TERESA: Baby you make a speech.

[Fez stood up.]

FEZ: Whatever we have been given, is a passing comfort

for life, and what we have is better and more lasting, for those who believe and put their trust in Allah.

TERESA: Praise the Lord.

[They all said Amen spontaneously.]

FEZ: I feel lucky to be in the company of such nice friends, I hope our wives friendship last for a long time. If it was not for their friendship, us men would not have met, rise your glasses, here's to us.

[They rise their glasses and drank. Yank stood up.]

YANK: Mi no so good at making speech, but mi remember reading in the good book, a good name is better than great wealth, and respect is better than silver or gold, rich and poor are found together, God has made them all.

ELENA: Praise the Lord.

[They said Amen spontaneously.]

YANK: Mi know good friends when mi meet them, and they are right here, raise yu glasses again.

[They rise their glasses again and drank. Misty is under the influence of alcohol, and in a romantic mood, she burst into poetry.]

MISTY: So we'll go no more a-rowing, so late into the night, though the heart be still as loving, and the moon be still as bright. For the sward out wears its sheath, and the soul wears out the breast, and the heart must pause to breathe, and love it self have rest. Though the night was made for loving, and the day returns too soon, yet we'll go no more a-rowing by the light of the moon.

ELENA: Who wrote that?

MISTY: It's one of Byron verses.

VICTOR: I remember one too! To be the father of the fatherless, to stretch the hand from the throne's height and raise his offspring, who expired in other days. To make thy sire's sway by a kingdom less, this is to be a monarch, and repress. Envy into unutterable praise. Dismiss thy guard, and trust thee to such traits, for who would lift a hand, except to bless. Were it not easy, sir, and is it not sweet. To make thyself beloved, and to be omnipotent by mercy's means, for thus thy sovereignty would grow but more complete. A despot thou, and yet people free, and by the heart, not hand enslaving us…. The

souls of the virtuous are in the hands of God.
[Yank and Elena are in their bedroom. The couple had just finish making passionate love making; they breath heavily, kiss and look at each other intensely.]

    YANK: Yu know yu pretty.

    ELENA: And you're a good lover. Yank

    YANK: Mmmm.

    ELENA: Mi been meaning to tell you some-thing.

    YANK: Yeah what!

[Elena wanted to tell Yank the truth, to confess her sin, because the stress laid on her was the danger of losing his love. The danger of losing the love of the super ego, carries the individual back to the debated problem of the sense of guilt.]

    ELENA: Remember when yu asked mi to marry yu.

    YANK: Ye!

    ELENA: Remember you though mi was pregnant?

    YANK: Yes... No what do yu mean thought!

    ELENA: Well... Mi was not pregnant at the time.

    ELENA: Would yu have asked mi to marry yu, if mi was not pregnant?

    YANK: Of course... Mi love yu... But what yu saying?

    ELENA: It was after yu asked mi to marry yu, mi tried to get pregnant.

    YANK: Mi see! That's why!

    ELENA: Yes that why Gibrel was a month late, it was after talking to Misty and Teresa, that mi realize how mi lie would fester and fester.

[Yank began shouting.]

    YANK: Yu mean yu tell them before yu tell mi!

[Yank ease him-self out the bed, still sitting he put on his dressing gown,, he walk to the light switch on the wall, and switch it on. He turn to face Elena and began walking up and down the room. Yank's feeling of transference neuroses, originate from the ego refusing to accept a powerful instinctual impulse in the id, his motor out let is to get out of bed. The ego defends itself against, the instinctual impulse by the mechanisms of repression. The repressed struggles against the fate.]

    ELENA: Don't shout yu'll disturb the neighbours!

    YANK: [shouting.] Mi no care bout the bloody neighbours.... What will they think a mi? They mean more to yu than mi do?

ELENA: [Elena pull the covers up and adjust her pillow.] No! It come out in conversation, and both of them think yu is a good man, it's a good job Gibrel is at mi parernts.

YANK: No tell mi fi stop shouting.

[Yank is feeling self conscious, he hide his face, he display anger for being scorn by Misty and Teresa; and worse of all being scorn by Fez and Victor friends he admires. He shows every signs of being bitterly hurt. He sit down in the bedroom chair.]

ELENA: What comes' after love?

YANK: Mi no know what yu mean!

[Elena protecting her super ego, the power of her destiny so that it has no longer any safeguard against all the dangers that surrounds it. That is the self-preservation of her love. We are hurt most by those we love most. In love there is perhaps always a fantasy, at lease of finding a close physical unity with the love one. Yank self esteem is broken, it is as painful as a physical wound. The self and the body is experienced as identical, both are hurt, the feeling of shame can convert into contempt.]

ELENA: What comes after intense sexual pleasure?

YANK: More sexual pleasure. [Yank admit to knowing the culture, he was brought up in, whilst he may not hold these opinions, he felt like being flippant.] What wrong with living in sin with a whole heap of pikny? Whole heap a people do it.

ELENA: [Calmly.] Now yu being stupid. So many black women have babies before they get married; mi was not brought up to hold those views, my education may be limited, but it does not mean mi not aware of the traps woman can fall into, mi have seen so many of mi school friends who get pregnant, after leaving school, only to be left on there own, only to meet another man and become pregnant again. As Misty would say, there reason are so common, peer pressure, it happen unconsciously, but it's also a way of asserting themselves as adults to their parents. Mi know yu love mi, was it only mi who wanted to share mi life with yu?

YANK: Mi ask yu to marry mi didn't mi. Mak yu tak so long to tell mi?

ELENA: Mi was so happy when mi was pregnant! And what with the wedding plans, mi became forgetful after Gibrel's birth, the sleepless nights! Breast feeding! Money worries! The bills! Remember mi hair dressing training, you were so good with Gibrel then!

YANK: So it no matter to yu, what if them tell Fez and Victor? [Elena momentarily felt intensely bad about what she had done. Once she had over come the fact of them being happily married, Elena could have told Yank, but some how it was never the right time. This was now made possible by the existence of her world of fantasy, of losing the love one and building trust, in the reality of their relationship.]

ELENA: Mi told them in confidence, mi don't think they will tell any one, coffee morning is like women time to talk bout things.

YANK: [Shouting.] Yu a tell mi sa mi no know woman?

ELENA: Misty and Teresa are mi friends, they're not just any women. Mi think they have a good understanding of human feelings.

YANK: Human feelings! Mi don't think yu know how mi feel.

ELENA: Tell mi how yu feel?

[Yank feels inferior about himself, but this shame can be denied in perceiving weakness in others, for it relieves him of feeling weak or incompetent. Blaming a love one is often frightening, so an individual will readily leap to the idea, that it was really his own fault. Blame is interjected into the self, interjection is a very common activity, it goes on daily when learning new skills from Fez and Victor. Very close to shame is the experience of guilt, both involves actual or fantasize awareness of being observe by others.]

YANK: Stupid mi pride hurt man.

ELENA: If it helps mi feel stupid too. Yank yu have to think of yu positives, yu have a skill job and yu lucky, yu never end up like some of those black men, who have babies for all three different women, some of them end up in prison for criminal behaviour.

[Yank get out of the bedroom chair, walk to the wall and switch off the light, then walk to the bed and take of his dressing gown, then get into bed.]

[Misty came to the conclusion, after a visit to The Glitzey Office one evening, that Victor is committing adultery; because of his attitude to spending money, and what she saw at the office. On these occasion Victor and Misty would stop in Greenwich for a drink in a pub. Misty wanted to hand in her assignment for the recipes, and to arrange with Justin, a time to take photographs of the dishes. Misty saw Victor from a distance, in the office, sitting on one of the journalist desk talking. Misty could not here their conversation. However the flirtatious manner of their conversation, made Misty felt suspicious of them. Misty's feelings of anxiety are understandable. It's easy enough to delude ourselves that we have no effect on others at all. Often unconscious, manipulation of gesture and position of the self, relative to other in the outside world, is one of the commonest of mental tricks.]

VICTOR: How did your interview went with Linford Christie? [Martha lean back on her chair, using both hands pulled her fingers through her long, blonde shoulder length hair, and pout her lips.]

MARTHA: It went well, he's such a hunk! Those muscles! [Victor lean forward as he spoke, to observe closely Martha's breast. He was going to ask her about her injury, he did not because he could see, it was a love bite on the top of her breast.]

VICTOR: Did you get the scoop?

MARTHA: Yes he gave me an in depth story, his feelings about his disciplinary proceeding, clearing him of steroid, his athletics career, his retirement from athletics, his school, education, family, and his broadcasting career.

VICTOR: Who was the photographer?

MARTHA: Justin. Oh excellent photographs of him, and home life.
[Victor sense the immediate danger of Martha's fraternization, he went to assert his position of authority, and reinforce the fact that the office was a place for work, not for pleasure of the flesh.. Religious yes, but he's a man of the world; as soon as possible, is a sarcastic comment.]

VICTOR: I want it on my desk ASAP.
[Misty did not stay to observe any more, she walked back through the door, LEFT. And saw the Editors Personal Assistant sitting at her desk.]

MISTY: Hand this to Victor for me, oh and ask Justin to contact me?

BETTY: Justin is out of the country on an assignment, and Victor Boaz is in the office Misses Boaz.

MISTY: It's ok I can't stop.
[Misty held back her tears and walk across the stage and left. RIGHT.]
[Elena is in the back seat of the car, Misty and Teresa are in the front seat, Teresa is driving. They are dress in tight T shirts, jodhpurs and ridding boots, Elena is wearing a tight fitting T shirt with a vent across the chest.]

TERESA: Guess what Fez brought me, after our meal out at Joanna's.
[Elena and Misty responded spontaneously.]

MISTY: What!

Amazing Caring Woman

ELENA: What!

TERESA: A ball and chain!

MISTY: I just imagine you in your bedroom, dress in sexy underwear, with Fez attaching to your ankle a ball and chain. What sort of ball and chain?

TERESA: It's a gold ankle bracelet, with a ball and chain.

MISTY: Oh my days! That's really nice, Victor is quite the miser these days, still, we had a romantic night when we got home, in fact he said in French, tes mains me fait sentir come un velous sur mon dos.

ELENA: What it mean in English?

[Misty turn to look at Elena, raise her eyebrows and smile.] My hands feel like silk down his back.

ELENA: A tell yu Yank was mighty when we got home…. A mi want a ball and chain, will one of yu baby sit for mi one evening?

TERESA: Yes we will baby sit, Why, where you're going?

ELENA: Yank pride is a little shattered, mi planning to cook him a meal, mi going to start with one of Rusty Lee callaloo fish soup, then jerk chicken, some thing for him to lick his fingers with, yam green bananas and a tropical fruit salad.

MISTY: Wow a romantic evening in for two how lovely!

ELENA: Yes mi think it will help.

MISTY: What wrong with his pride?

ELENA: Well after the meal out mi finely found the courage, to tell him about Gibrel's conception. We made love and sort of made up. But he did not take it too well.

TERESA: I see you mean his male ego thing.

ELENA: Yes.

MISTY: Men and their ego, I don't know.

ELENA: Yu both have not told any-one, about what mi told yu at coffee morning did yu?

[Teresa and Misty responded spontaneously.]

MISTY: Nooo!

TERESA: Nooo!

ELENA: Yank was hurt because mi told yu first, him think woman are chatter box, and you're likely to tell every body.

MISTY: Oh no! It's a sensitive issue and its not some thing I would disclose to any one.

TERESA: You mean he is sensitive!

ELENA: It not just being sensitive, he feels Victor and Fez would not respect him if they know.

TERESA: I have not told Fez, I didn't think it was a problem, Gibrel is his son and you both love each other.

MISTY: He sees Victor and Fez as men who would do the right thing, when it come to marriage.

TERESA: Men are men no matter how intelligent they are, give them an inch and they take a yard, they all have their weak points.

MISTY: Yes you're right!

TERESA: You tell him from us, that Fez and Victor would not think disrespectful of him. Would you agree Misty? Misty you seem far away!

[Misty in deep thought.]

MISTY: Yes yes I agree.

[They got out the car with their ridding hats in their hand, and start walking off the stage, Misty stop. LEFT.]

MISTY: I will catch you up. [Misty talking to her self.] I feel so stupid for not having confronted Victor, about what I saw in the office. I'm afraid to hear the truth. It's so humiliating, to think of discussing it with Martha, let along the senior colleagues. There is something going on between them, and they must be colluding with him! Well if he has found another love, he will leave me any way, and it's not me to fight over him in public. I'm going to think thing over, I wish I heard what they were saying ; I going to heal my wounds, today I'm going to rise above it, and enjoy horse ridding. [She walk off the stage. LEFT.]

[LEFT. They are walking the horses.]

ELENA: Lorraine, will you take us around the golf course this time?

LORRAINE: Yes it's one of the best ride.

TERESA: Elena where did you get your T-shirt?

ELENA: Peacock.

TERESA: Oh!

LORRAINE: Don't forget to squeeze with your knees, when

we go into a trot; and keep your bottom on the saddle, straight backs. [Lorraine lead the way across the stage, turning back across the stage they began to trot, when Lorraine stop they stop, they are in a good mood, as they walk the horses across the stage. Misty began singing, Teresa and Elena join in, the song is by Simple Red. Two men came on to the stage with golf clubs. RIGHT. The rapturous way the women look, made the two middle age men to stop playing golf, and look at them, and hit the golf ball with no particular aim.

MISTY: It's only love doing it's thing, it's only love it's only love, don't be afraid to touch me bab, girl it's been real, there nothing wrong with the way you carry on, so enjoy and live because it's only love doing it's thing baby, it's only love that you feeling, girl you feeling, it's only love doing it's thing baby it's only love that you giving. [They trot again then stop, and start to walk the horses.]

MISTY: It's nice here?

TERESA: Oooh yes! I wander if it would be just as nice, to be ridding in a tropical country?

MISTY: Mmm yes! I see what you mean.

ELENA: Some time mi think Teresa is more West Indian than us.

TERESA: Well, mi great great grand father had settled in the West Indies; I believe he was from one of the Scandinavian countries. I think he must have travelled from Island to Island, because the Leeward Islands, still have white settlers there, who originated from Scandinavia.

ELENA: Mi often wandered how Teresa look more white looking, of the mixed race, and the way yu can slip into patois!

TERESA: Although my parents have lost their accent, when they speak on the phone to relative in Saint Lucia, they often slip in to patois. What they have shared with me about Saint Lucia, have help me a great deal; when it come to communicating with the elderly at the Calabash. A lot of them think it's quite funny when they here me break into patois.

MISTY: Do you think there is a lot more mix marriages in the Leeward Islands?

TERESA: Yes I think so, from what I understand from my parents, their relatives have learnt to mix, some are in mix marriages, and those who own business have a rapór with their customers, who are black Caribbean.

ELENA: They have been mixing in Jamaica, since the discovery of the Arawak Indians; there are some white people there, who have managed to cut them selves off from the native population.

TERESA: Who are they?

ELENA: White Germans.

MISTY: I would like to meet both your parents some day?

TERESA: Yes it's a good idea.

ELENA: What do your parents do? And how did you become a Senior Press Officer?

MISTY: My Mother is a Senior Publicity Officer for the BBC, and my Father is a Team Leader for Social Workers.

ELENA: Wow!

MISTY: There is a gap between us siblings, my brother Cloud is the Publishing Director for The Glitzey, he's thirty-eight, Sky is thirty-two, I'm the youngest.

TERESA: Does Cloud work in the same office as Victor?

MISTY: No there office is some where else. When I was a teenager I became involved in an amateur theatre company, I help making the costumes, and I was the script prompter. I started writing short stories for a local news paper, when I was doing my 'A' levels, and I did a degree in journalism.

TERESA: Met any more famous people?

MISTY: Oh yes. Albert Finney, Tom Courtney, Felicity Kendal and Anthony Newley. What a shy man he is, for such an experience actor. The theatre production are often of the classics, Dickens, Shakespeare and John Osborne. There are repertoire of other productions, there is a show of the Merchant Of Venice at the moment. I'm arranging for Gabrielle Jordon and Henry Goodman, to go on television to promote the theatre play.

ELENA: Mi would like to see it! Could yu get us some tickets?

TERESA: So would I!

MISTY: Yes of course.

TERESA: I'm going to call in at Fez Video, Misty would you like

to come with me?
>   MISTY: Yes.
>   ELENA: Drop mi back at mi shop first.

ACT TWO

[Patricia is typing the invoices into the computer, Teresa and Misty enter. LEFT.]
    TERESA: Hi pat.
    PATRICIA: Hello Teresa.
    TERESA: This is my friend Misty, her husband is the Editor of The Glitzey.
    PATRICIA: Aaaa nice to meet you, it's a good magazine.
    MISTY: Nice to meet you too.
    PATRICIA: [In a huff.] Now Teresa I would like you to have a word with Fez, because I'm the dog's body around here, he's not going to get me to edit those things. I don't mind doing the gardens, weddings, and christenings, but it's those other things I object to.
    TERESA: What other things! Aaaa the light on it means they are editing, and they are not to be disturb, Misty could you wait here.
    MISTY: Yes of course.
[Teresa went through a door leading to the reception area, there is a table stage right and a door to the right, facing her is two editing suit, the lights goes on when Teresa enter the suit and start talking to them.]
    PATRICIA: Would you like a cup of tea? Please sit down.
[Misty sit down on a chair.]
    MISTY: Yes please.
[Patricia enter the door to the reception area, and went through the door to the kitchenette. RIGHT.]
[Teresa enter Fez editing suite, she hope to surprise him, and was surprise by noise of sexual noise making. Fez and Yank are standing in front of two video screen monitors; Teresa saw a glimpse of the video. The video was an explicit scene of two people copulating, penis going into the virginal. Fez and Yank immediately turn around as Teresa enter, they look at her with a shock expression. Fez stopped the video, and switch of the screen monitors, the men were like two naughty boys caught in the act of bad behaviour. Teresa blurted.]
    TERESA: What's going on here!
    YANK: [Yank feeling awkward quickly left the room.] Mi better go and

finish your repair. [Yank went to the reception area, and went under the table, where he start to the electrical repair, of fixing a new electric socket.] [Patricia return to her desk, holding a cup of tea, she gave the tea to Misty, and sip her tea.]

PATRICIA: Editing is not as easy as it seems, I'm paid for each video I edit, it's a good top up, but these days I'm not so keen on editing, those things make nudist camp look decent, and the Jerry Springer show look tolerable, the ones where they turn up on the show half naked; the rest are people with no values! It's like a modern day Roman Arena. [Misty open her mouth again to speak, but was silenced by Patricia continual talking.]

PATRICIA: I'm not a prude, I have children, but I like to go to bed and have nice dreams, especially after editing one of those gardens, with those soft petals, the shapely and colourful leaves of the trees and shrubs, with the clam classical music; and the beautiful weddings, not left with those memories of groaning. He won't find another like me, all this administration, reception, editing. [Patricia smiling.] Course he trained me to do the editing. If my Stan know about this, I would have to leave, I mean he would not want me to work here.

MISTY: Do you like the work?

PATRICIA: Oh yes, it's a small business but it keeps me occupied, and it help to pay for our holidays, social activities, and it keeps my car on the road. Fancy taking on those jobs! I suppose he needs the money, what with over heads and things.

[The light goes off where Patricia and Misty is and goes on in Fez video suite.] [Fez is not only caught by his wife, but his receptionist had already made it clear about her opinion. His fears are the result of anxieties, these arise from the mere fact of what is not considered socially healthy behaviour. It a crisis affecting the integration of the ego; when ever this sense is lost, when ever integrity yields to despair and disgust. Fez speaking softly.]

FEZ: Don't get miserable on me.

[Teresa feels she is married to a deviant, his behaviour does not conform to social expectation. She feels he has departed from social norms, she is primarily concerned with protecting their reparation, and the reparation of those they know, love and respect. Teresa in a angry voice.]

TERESA: You're an enigma! [Often when confronted with unexpected and unacceptable behaviour, we say he must be sick or what's wrong with him, not all behaviour is conformist, a sense of identity is achieved primarily, through the individual's complete surrender, to give into social norms, and through his unconditional adaptation to the demands made upon him.]

FEZ: Don't get hysterical I'm not that sick. [Conscientious discipline is intrinsic to any work. It seems that work must be rewarded, by money in Fez case, for his devilish behaviour.]

FEZ: It's a thousand pounds for one edit. [Said with a little relief from fear of revulsion, although there is a little neurotic pleasure in his suffering.]

TERESA: What!

FEZ: It's only one client I'm editing them for.

[Teresa regard Fez behaviour as in comprehensible, even weird, however his behaviour is a result of imperfection, of trying to spur toward paying of a loan. Work without recompense is not conceivable.]

TERESA: I still think it's vulgar, we are suppose to be running a respectable business.

FEZ: It's helping to pay of a loan. [There is some animosity between them.]

TERESA: We will talk about this later, I got Misty out in the front entrance, I would like to show her around the business. [Fez getting into a fluster took out the video from the control unit, and replaced it with another video.

TERESA: What about Azaziah editing suite?

FEZ: This is the only one. [Fez and Teresa left the editing suite, to the reception area.]

FEZ: How are you getting on Yank?

YANK: Who mi, mi soon finish.

[They walk through the door to the front entrance.]

FEZ: Aaaa Misty, salam alai kun.

MISTY: Alai kun salam.

FEZ: It will give me great pleasure to show you around.

MISTY: Great! Patricia has been very hospitable, I have been told editing is not as easy as it seems.

[Fez and Teresa glared at Patricia and hurry Misty into the reception area. Misty observe the animosity between them, having a idea of what it's about, she felt it best to avoid discussing the matter. Patricia began typing into the computer. Yank was humming to himself when they came in, he came out from under the table.

YANK: Kiss mi neck a Misty!

MISTY: Hi Yank you seem cheerful.

YANK: A happy mak mi awaan so.

TERESA: We are showing Misty around the business.

YANK: Seeing is believing.

[Fez and Teresa look at Yank timidly.]

FEZ: These two rooms are the editing suite, Azaziah works in this suite. [Pointing to the left suite.]

[The light went on in Azaziah suite as they enter, he was editing scenes on a training video for a foot ball team. He turn around look at them, and did a double look at Misty.]

FEZ: Azaziah don't let me interrupt you, I'm just showing a friend around.

AZAZIAH: Aaaa yes!

FEZ: Don't think about it she is married.

[Azaziah turn to face the control unit, replayed the screen where a foot ball player kick the ball into the net. He turn to look at them again.]

AZAZIAH: What a goal What!

MISTY: It sure was! What a lot of equipment, is it complicated to operate?

FEZ: I'll show you in the next suite. [They left the suite and enter Fez suite.]

TERESA: This is where Fez does his editing.

[Misty had a good look around at the equipment, on the floor to one corner is a prayer rug rolled up, and a shelf with books on it.] [Yank shout to say he leaving, and go out the door to the entrance area, with his tool bag. LEFT]

YANK: Leaving now bye.

FEZ: Bye Yank, basically Misty this is post production, the video tape editing unit consists of these components, the video tape player, recorder, and editing control unit, and the screen monitors. The monitors show scene from the master tape, allowing me to preview scenes, once located I then edit them together.

MISTY: This is very interesting!

FEZ: Would you like me to show you a tape?

MISTY: Yes please.

[Fez load a tape into the video tape player, of Harniman Museum Gardens, and press the player button.]

MISTY: I recognize the garden!

TERESA: It's Harniman Gardens.

FEZ: Well that it, it just these two suite, the room where Yank is working, is where the tape are labelled and dated, and the entrance area where Patricia is, and a wash room and kitchenette.

MISTY: Who is your clients?

FEZ: I have contracts with various organizations, shops, offices, sports teams, Borough Councils, other clients are for weddings and christenings. Hope you will tell Victor about the business, I sure would like a column written about the business in The Glitzey.

MISTY: The Glitzey features articles on successful businesses for African and Caribbean people, in todays British society. I'm sure Victor will talk to Alistair Bolton, the Feature Editor about your business. I will remind him again. Look I must go now, I'd like to do a little shopping before I head for home.

[Fez show Misty to the front entrance, LEFT]

MISTY: Bye Patricia.

PATRICIA: Bye Misty nice meeting you.

FEZ: Bye take care.

MISTY: I will bye.

[Fez return to his editing suite.]

TERESA: Fez I want you to think seriously, about giving up editing those video?

FEZ: Teresa I said it paying off a loan.

[Fez sat down at the control unit and began editing a sport video, Teresa is standing beside him.] [Teresa sigh.]

TERESA: You are good at editing, but those videos!

[Teresa walk away from Fez, she look at the self of books, pick up his Holy Quran, she open it, turn a page and began to read, in a calm and gentle voice, Fez listen..

TERESA: Allah will bring them into his mercy, Lo! Allah is forgiving, merciful; and the first to lead the way, of the Muhajirin and the Ansar, and those who followed them in goodness. Allah is well pleased with him; and he hath made ready for them, gardens underneath where rivers flow, where in they will abide for ever. That is the supreme triumph. And there are others who have acknowledge their faults; they mixed a righteous action with another that was bad.

It may be that Allah will relent toward them. Lo! Allah is relenting merciful.
[Fez got up out of his chair, walk over to Teresa, kiss her on the lips, they hug, he look up. We most allow the word of God to correct us, the same way we allow it to encourage us.]

FEZ: I will tell the client, this is the last one. [Teresa look at him, they kiss.]

TERESA: Thanks.

[There are three compartment on stage, one with a desk, chair, telephone and door to the left. Behind the door is a desk, chair and telephone and computer. In the middle is kitchen with a table and chairs, To the right is two doors, a hotel sofa, side table, telephone, chair and small table. The light goes on for each act.] [Victor is on the telephone is talking on the telephone to one of Whitney Houston travelling companion.]

LOUISE: Miss Houston can't come to the phone right now. [Miss Houston enter the room. RIGHT.]

WHITNEY HOUSTON: Who is it? [Louise put her hand over the mouth-piece of the telephone.]

LOUISE: It's a man name Victor Boaz, from The Glitzey, it's a magazine.

WHITNEY HOUSTON: I'll take It. [Whitney walk over to Louise and take the telephone from her.]

WHITNEY HOUSTON: Victor Boaz, what can I do for you?

VICTOR: It's a great pleasure to speak to you Miss Houston. The Glitzey would love to write a story on you?

WHITNEY HOUSTON: Look Mister Boaz, I'm to take a flight out the country tomorrow.

VICTOR: Miss Houston you're the undisputed, most popular black female singer of all time, and a movie star, and our readers here in Britain would be thrilled to read about you in The Glitzey.

WHITNEY HOUSTON: The Glitzey, I've not heard of it!

VICTOR: The Glitzey is a new magazine on the market, it specialize in African and Caribbean people, in todays British society; our readers would love to read your story, may I call you Whitney?

WHITNEY HOUSTON: It's cool.

VICTOR: You have a stunning voice, and you're a stunning vocalist.

WHITNEY HOUSTON: Thank you.

VICTOR: The Glitzey is willing to pay a substantial sum for a story. You're a famous African American, you should appreciate us black British struggles.

WHITNEY HOUSTON: A story!

VICTOR: Whitney, I can get one of our Journalist and Photographer, to the Hilton Hotel, Park Lane in one hour. Journalism is often like this.

WHITNEY HOUSTON: You have a cool British accent Victor, why can't you get the story and clue me into The Glitzey?

[Victor hesitate because he is not expecting her, to ask him to conduct the interview.]

VICTOR: I'm the Editor. Whitney, for you and this story I will join them.

WHITNEY HOUSTON: See you soon Victor. [Miss Houston Put the telephone back in its holder.]

[Victor make two more telephone calls, to the Photographer and Journalist.]

NOLAN: Hello.

VICTOR: Nolan meet me at the Hilton Hotel, Park Lane in an hour.

NOLAN: See you there.

[Victor press the disconnect button and press the extension button to the Journalist office.]

JEFFREY: Hello.

VICTOR: Jeffrey drop every-thing meet me at reception promote. [Victor put some paper in his brief case, pick up his cell phone to make a call, then change his mind and put the phone back on his desk, he grab his jacket, he forgets his cell phone, and walk through the door to his Personal Assistant office.]

VICTOR: Betty phone my wife and tell her I going to be late. We are going to the Hilton Hotel, we're getting a story on Whitney Houston.

BETTY: Will do Mister Boaz. [Victor leave stage LEFT.] [Betty receive an emergency telephone call from her father, she pick up the telephone.]

DANIEL: Betty love, your mother is in Saint Thomas hospital, they suspect the worse, I'll meet you there. [Betty is in shock, tears is running from her eyes.]

BETTY: Oh no dad, I'll be there. [Betty forget to telephone Misses Boaz she put down the telephone, grab her hand bag and jacket, and leave stage LEFT.]

[Misty is dress in a neat attire, she finish laying the table, she put one candle in the centre of the flower arrangement.; and take a sip of wine., she look at her watch .]

MISTY: Seven forty five, where is he.

[In Whitney Houston suite, there is a table with a light supper for her guest. Victor and Jeffrey is helping them selves to some food. Nolan is taking photographs of Whitney Houston.]

NOLAN: Miss Houston you look stunning, can I get a photo of you relaxing in the settee?

[Whitney Houston walk over to the settee and adapt a relaxing poise in the settee.]

VICTOR: As I was saying Whitney, The Glitzey has been in the shops for a year. It's similar to the Ebony.

NOLAN: Say hot chocolate, hold that smile. [Nolan took several photographs.]

WHITNEY HOUSTON: You read the Ebony over here?

VICTOR: We sure do.

WHITNEY HOUSTON: So cool!

[Misty pick up her cell phone and call Victor's cell phone, he does not answer his phone, she disconnect the call, and put the phone down on the table.]

MISTY: Where could he be, he's not answering his phone! [No matter how intelligent, beautiful or from what ever racial background, a woman when threaten in love, will explode or revert to irrational behaviour, and sink into utter despair. She put the lettuce in the salad spinner and start spinning them.]

MISTY: He's seeing her that's it. [Misty take the chopping board out of the cupboard, and the box grater, and began to grater a carrot, she put the carrot on the plate with the lettuce and tuna fish. She walk to the refrigerator and take two hot scotch bonnet pepper out, and walk to the pot on the stove, pick up the lid, and drop the two pepper in the pot. That should do it two hot scotch bonnet pepper. She put the lid back on the pot, and get her plate and walk to sit at the kitchen table, she began to eat and drink her wine, she then began to cry, she wipe the tears with her hand. She then pick up her cell phone and press a number.]

GEORGE: Hello.

MISTY: Hello George, please forgive me if I have call at an inconvenient time.

GEORGE: No trouble Misty, what can I do for you?

MISTY: It's Victor, I've tried his cell phone several times, and he does not answer, I'm worried, do you know what time he left the office?

GEORGE: Come to think about it, I did not see him leave the office.

MISTY: I've tried the office, there is no one there.

GEORGE: Look Misty, I'm sure he will be home soon, he's probably playing squash with Alistair.

MISTY: Thanks George, bye for now.

GEORGE: Bye Misty.

[Misty disconnect her cell phone, and put it down on the table.]

MISTY: This is not like Victor, he would have let me know!

[In Whitney Houston suite, she is in another change of clothe; and is sitting in the settee. Nolan was taking photographs, Jeffrey is sitting on a chair next to the settee, asking questions with his note pad and pen; and Victor is drinking and talking quietly with Louise, Nolan join them.]

JEFFREY: Miss Houston, you have worked with your rival Mariah Carey, tell me, how did you get on?

WHITNEY HOUSTON: People think Mariah assume my position as queen of pop, by using a similar style. There is no rift between us; when I had spoken to Mariah, I say hi how are you doing. We worked together on the song 'When You Believe', from the sound track for the animated film, The Prince of Egypt.

JEFFREY: Would you say it was challenging?

WHITNEY HOUSTON: Yes, but I enjoyed it.

JEFFREY: You are clearly a committed mother, what's your opinion on bring Bobby Kristina in the world of stardom?

WHITNEY HOUSTON: We just want to keep her ahead in the perspective. We don't want her to drink the perfume, we just want her to smell it, get a whiff of it.

JEFFREY: Thanks Miss Houston. I'm all done here. Victor I'm finish.

[Victor walk over to Miss Houston and shake her hand, Nolan and Jeffery walk out the door. RIGHT.]

VICTOR: Thank you. [They both walk to the door.] Thank you again, I will send you a magazine with your story, bye.

[Whitney Houston nodding.]

WHITNEY HOUSTON: That will be cool.

[Victor leave the suite, Nolan pop his head around the door.]

Amazing Caring Woman

NOLAN: The camera loves you.

[Misty is sitting at the kitchen table drinking wine and reading the guardian news paper, she put down the news paper, and look at her watch, it is showing ten thirty; she is almost pulling her hair out with anxiety. She get up out of the chair, and walk up and down the kitchen. She pick up her cell phone and press the number to **Natasha**, the Art Director for The Glitzey.]

MISTY: Ten thirty,

NATASHA: Hello.

MISTY: Hello Natasha, please forgive me for calling so late, but did you see Victor leave the office this evening?

NATASHA: Yes, come to think of it I did; he was talking to Jeffrey. Victor did leave quite suddenly!

MISTY: I don't know why I did not think of phoning you earlier, thanks Natasha, I'm worried,

NATASHA: At our next editors' meeting, I'm going to suggest we all should make our where about be known.

[Misty is asleep in their bedroom, it's midnight.] [Victor open the bedroom door and enter, he walk over to the bed and switch on the light. Misty woke up and sit up. LEFT.]

MISTY: What happen to you?

[Victor is on an emotional high, and a little drunk from drinking with **Nolan** and **Jeffery**, he is excited for having got a story from an American star; he did not really caught on to what **Misty** said, he started to take off his jacket and tie. As he is talking, he open the wardrobe, and put away his jacket and tie,

VICTOR: Great evening! The magazine should be a sell out for the next two months. With stories on King Ronald Muwenda Mutebi and Queen Sylvia! Home Office Minister Paul Boateng! Linford Christie! And Whitney Houston!

MISTY: Whitney Houston how did you!

[Victor walk to the double arm chaise, sat down and take of his shoes and socks, he look at his watch.]

VICTOR: It was all very sudden, Whitney Houston is staying at the Hilton Hotel Park Lane, she is due a flight out today. I managed to persuade her to give The Glitzey a story. Nolan took some stunning photographs!

MISTY: How exciting! Why didn't you let me know?

VICTOR: Didn't.

MISTY: I was worried crazy, George and Natasha didn't know where you were.
[Victor started to unbutton his shirt, he stop and was about to say some-thing when Misty lash out angrily.]
MISTY: You're like the straw that breaks the camel's back, I saw you fraternizing with Martha in the office, now you turn up late, no message, leaving me to fret about you, and you're being very tight with money, we have not gone any where together for weeks.
VICTOR: That's odd! I told Betty to let you know I was going to be late.
MISTY: [Angrily.] She didn't.
VICTOR: What's this about Martha!
MISTY: I saw you together yesterday, I brought the recipes in, what was it all about.
VICTOR: The thing with Martha, is her adrenaline goes sky high, when she's out on a story. She is a skilled journalist. [Victor finish unbutton his shirt, he take it off to reveal his naked upper body.]
MISTY: Why were you peeping down her blouse?
VICTOR: She strike me as being so youthful, as to display a love bite on the top of her breast!
MISTY: So Natasha was right, when she said Martha was wandering around the office, with a love bite for every-one to see.
VICTOR: Misty, life is made up of different people, with varying personalities, many are respected because of the values they hold.
MISTY: Why couldn't one of the journalist go on the story?
VICTOR: Whitney Houston wanted me to clue her in about The Glitzey. It was worth getting the story; Jeffrey did the interview. My love you meet famous people?
[Misty feels she needs to remind Victor that she is a professional, and is able to make good judgement about personalities.]
MISTY: They are talented egotistic souls, who's profession is the stage, there are those who live for God.
[Victor walks up and down the room.]
VICTOR: I have not kept it a secret from those in the office of my faith, I hope they see me as a God fearing man; those who have respect for God, should show respect for me, it's not other people's

mistakes we live by, or their evil ways, but the strength in the laws and commandment we have come to know and love.
[From Biblical terms each one of us needs, to use the knowledge gained by others before us, but we also have to discover every-thing a new for our selves, and practice it. Only through practice can we really believe what we feel and know. What's more, we must not forget that we are so prone to self deception; so we need to be critically aware of our tricks of thought. Also our effect on others, if a stable climate of understanding is to be cultivated.] [Victor not knowing what happen to Betty's mother, felt betrayed by his colleagues in the office.]

VICTOR: Experience tells me this is not like Betty, logic tell me some-thing went wrong, could it be the telephone lines went dead. [Victor tells Misty she is beautiful when angry in Spanish, hoping it would sound more appealing to her, Misty softens at his complement.]

VICTOR: Tu es bonita quando tu es entaldu. What's this all about?
[This paucity of words, I'm feeling broody, during her quiet, sad statement, is commenting on another unanswered question of money. Rudeness, inconsiderate, or lack of respect are not the things that bind their relationship. She needed to know what he had done with their nest egg.]

MISTY: I guess I'm feeling broody, and I think you're not ready. [Victor is standing by the door, Misty gets out of bed and walks to leave the room, she brushed pass him. He held her by the arm and pulled her back to him.]

VICTOR: I would be upset if you were not worried about me.

MISTY: I'm worried about us, would you like to tell me what you have done with five thousand pounds? [She pulled away from him.]
[Victor wanted to surprise her about his plan for their holiday, he could not hold out any longer, he had to tell her.]

VICTOR: I'm going to book fights for us to go to Saint Vincent, the hotel is one of the best on the island.

MISTY: [look at him and softens.] You surprise me.
[Victor pull her to him, she could not resist his masculine embrace, she look softly in his eyes, they kiss a deep passionate kiss.
[There is two squash court one for the men, the other the women, to the right of the stage is bench where Teresa is sitting. The lights goes on for each act, they are talking whilst playing.]

MISTY: It's been well over a month since we last saw each other, how have things been with you?

ELENA: Things have been fine, except mi had a difficult customer this week, you know how long it takes, to get our hair curly permed.

MISTY: Yes.

ELENA: Well you know, mi like to have a little chat with mi customers.

MISTY: Yes.

ELENA: It so happened, this customer had two parking tickets in one week, a fine of one hundred and eighty pounds! She was stressed out mi tell yu! When mi took the rollers out her hair, it didn't curled!

MISTY: Oh, after all those hours!

ELENA: Yes she was loud, she refused to pay, she refused to return to have her hair redone, she looked in the mirror, touching her uncurled hair and said. 'But see ya, mi hair mash up'. And walked out.

MISTY: You're lucky you didn't get a letter from the consumer commission.

ELENA: Mi did follow her out the shop, and tried to explain that stress, could well be the cause.

MISTY: So being a hair dresser does have it's ups and downs.

ELENA: Yu telling mi.

[Victor and Fez are playing squash. They are playing their last game. Fez is running to get the ball, he hits' himself against the wall, somersault back-wards on the squash court floor, he get up.]

FEZ: I never realized it would have happen so quickly!

VICTOR: I have being reading about things like sleepless nights!

FEZ: Have you come to a decision about writing a column in The Glitzey about my business?

VICTOR: I will be sending one of my Journalist and Photographer soon, I want you to emphasize on your African heritage.

[Fez leaves the squash court and sit on the bench next to Teresa, she gives him a bottle water, he drink it. Yank take his turn on the squash court. They play a vigorous game, they are both sweating, but Yank is exuding sweat.]

YANK: Mi see this ya game on television, never dream mi would a da ya and a sweat buckets so!

VICTOR: Sky and Bauer barbeque is in two months time.

YANK: Aaaa yeah, Misty's Sister, wi will come, can wi bring Gibrel?

VICTOR: Yes other children will be there, they have two of their own, I think it's on a Sunday afternoon.

YANK: Wi haf fi bring any thing?

VICTOR: Just a bottle.

[Fez and Teresa are watching the game, they are drinking bottle water.]

TERESA: They are playing a good game?

FEZ: They sure are.

[Victor and Yank are hot sweaty and breathless.]

YANK: Good news bout Fez and Teresa?

VICTOR: Yes it is.

YANK: Dem no joke when it come to making baby!

VICTOR: You're right there!

YANK: Mi wander what they will have, boy or girl.

VICTOR: We will ask them what they would prefer.

[Victor hit the ball hard on the wall, Yank had to make a great effort to hit his return shot.]

YANK: When yu going to start fi yu family?

VICTOR: We are working on it.

YANK: Teresa so maga, mi sure she will be fussing bout putting on weight.

VICTOR: Did Elena fussed about putting on weight?

YANK: Ye! Woman them fuss bout every thing.

[Elena is frantically running to hit the ball, she ends up all over the squash court floor.]

ELENA: Give mi horse ridding any day, out there in the open air, letting the horse do all the work.

MISTY: I'm sorry to hear about Yank's grand aunt.

ELENA: It came as a shock to the family. [They sighed.]

ELENA: It was a massive stroke.

MISTY: Aaaa it's sad, did she have any children?

ELENA: Yes one daughter, Sonia, she lives in a council flat; with her two children. Grand Aunt Marcia was Yank Mum Aunt. Sonia and her children will be fine, they have been left the house in her will.

MISTY: That's good!

ELENA: Yes, Yank was left the household possession.

MISTY: Really! Any Chippendale, Riesner, or Mackintosh?

ELENA: [Stop and put her hand on her hip, and look at Misty.] Yu joking! [They laugh slightly.] [Misty and Elena are hot sweaty and tired, they are now playing at a slower pace.]

ELENA: It's a tree bedroom old house, and it needs' renovating, Sonia asked Yank to leave the curtains and carpets, and she will give him two hundred, when she have it. Yank sold the rest to a second hand shop.

MISTY: Did he get much for them?

ELENA: The men came with a van, and them took every-thing. Them packed every-thing from the cabinet into boxes, glasses crockery, them even took the crochet table mats. In the attic there was an old tin bath, two old paraffin heaters, and an old sowing machine, that have not be used in long time. Yank tried to get a thousand out of them, in the end he settled for nine hundred.

MISTY: Aaaa well is better than nothing.

ELENA: Mmmm. Although he was willed what was in the house, he had to give his Mother and Sonia some of the family photographers, they were hanging on the wall. Yank didn't want any thing from the spare rooms, one was rented out, the other, Sonia's children had sleep in at weekends and school holidays, the beds told a story of wet, wet, wet.

[Misty laugh.]

ELENA: Yank a doing some rewiring for her, Sonia want him to knock down the alcove, she say when she move in, she will do the rest bit by bit; it keeps' Yank busy a few evenings and some weekends.

MISTY: The funeral?

ELENA: Them bury her already.

[It is a Sunday afternoon, Victor and Misty had been to their Church, they are dress in their Sunday best. Victor had taken off his jacket, they are sitting in the settee, reading the Sunday paper, Misty is reading the Sunday review. Their Jerusalem Bible, Hertz Haftorahs and Apocrypha is on the coffee table.]

MISTY: Victor listen to this, I would like to go to this gallery.
[Victor put his paper down, and look over Misty shoulder as she read the review.]

MISTY: The sixteen century Dutch painter Jan Mostaert had wider horizons than most of his contemporaries, frequently taking on subjects from a new world, he can never have seen at first hand. Portrait of a moor reflects this interest. The calmness and objectivity of the picture, is typical of Dutch portraiture of the time, of which Mostaert was a supreme exponent. Appointed painter to Margaret of Austria Regent of the Netherlands, Mostaert pick up many commission from her courtiers. Unseen by the public for forty years, the picture is one of fifteen old masters in private collections, that have just come on the long term loan, to English Heritage for their Kenwood, House Gallery in North London.

[Just be for Misty stopped reading, Victor put his hand under the settee, and pull out airline tickets and brochure, and drop them in Misty's lap.]

MISTY: What's this! [Misty pick up tickets and read it.]

MISTY: Fight details for Victor Boaz and Misty Boaz to Saint Vincent, my goodness Victor! What a truly lovely, incredible thing you have done. [Misty look at him and kiss him, she then sat on his lap, and hug him, they kiss.]

VICTOR: I hope it will be a breath-taking holiday.

MISTY: It will be sensational! [Misty looking at the brochure.]

MISTY: Where is the location and hotel?

[Victor show her the location and hotel in the brochure.]

MISTY: It look expensive. [Misty kiss Victor.]

MISTY: I'm going to get lunch ready. [Misty gets out of the settee, and leave the room. RIGHT. The door bell ring, Victor gets out of the settee and walk to open the door. LEFT.]

VICTOR: Good afternoon Yank, come in come in.

[Yank is wearing his work clothes, he has two painting under his arm, they are wrap in old news paper.]

YANK: Thanks. [They walk and stand by the coffee table.]

YANK: Mi want yu honest opinion, bout these paintings, mi think yu have a yai fi art?

[Yank unwrapped the paintings, Victor took one of them and look at it.]

YANK: Are yu going out?

VICTOR: No we've been to church. [Victor put down the painting on the coffee table, and took the other painting from Yank and look at it.]

VICTOR: These are marvelous, long horns I believe, ingenious piece of work!

YANK: Some one seem to be obsess with cows, don't yu think?

[Misty come into the room.]

MISTY: Who was at the door? Aaaa Yank! How are you?

YANK: Mi fine Misty.

MISTY: Elena and Gibrel?

YANK: They are fine too.

[Misty left the room and went back into the kitchen.]

VICTOR: Would you like a drink?

YANK: Mi wi have a lager if yu got one.

VICTOR: [He is looking at the paintings, shouting, Misty love, could we have a couple of lagers, out the fridge; where did you get them?

YANK: Mi no mind telling yu, mi did a do some work in a house fi mi cousin Sonia; them was behind the alcove, wa mi knocked down.

VICTOR: From what I hear about the will, they are yours. [Picking up the painting.] This one is painted by someone named Hurt. [Putting it down and picking up the other painting.] And this one, I think the name look like Percy.

MISTY: [Misty brought the lager on a tray with two glasses. She put them on the small table next to the settee.] Aaa paintings, they are lovely, I'm not stopping I have something on the cooker. [She left the room. Victor and Yank open the cans of lager, and began drinking from the can, They sat down and relax in the settee.]

VICTOR: I think they could be worth something, the scenery is dramatic!

YANK: Really! Yu think so.

VICTOR: It's interesting how you found them.

YANK: Why?

VICTOR: In ancient times it was customary, for men to hide there treasures. The earth was thought to be a safe place, robberies were frequent, especially when ever there was war or a change in the ruling power.

YANK: Yu mean like Treasure Island?

[Victor nodded although he felt Treasure Island is fiction he felt Yank obtain the drift of what he was talking about.]

YANK: Mi read it man, mi read it.

VICTOR: As a consequence the rich endeavor to preserve their wealth by concealing them.

YANK: Wa mak yu say concealing them?

VICTOR: Jewelry, furniture, fine arts, are all part of their wealth.

YANK: Mi see.

VICTOR: The earth was looked upon as a safe hiding place; often the place of concealment was forgotten.

YANK: So yu think the paintings could have been da for a century?

VICTOR: I'm not sure how old they are. It's possible, imprisonment or exile often separate them from their treasure. The trouble of taking such pains to conceal them, are often left for the fortunate finder.

YANK: What yu suggest mi do with them? [They drink some more of their lager.]

VICTOR: They are fine quality paintings, and if I were you, I would take them to Sotheby's.

YANK: Mi was thinking to tak them to one junk shop! To see if mi could get a hundred fi them. Yu think yu could tak them there fi mi? Them stoosh.

VICTOR: I have a few editorial issues to, not forgetting an ad for a new journalist, they are such an interesting find, I'm sure they are worth something. [Shouting.] Misty love, come here a minute. [Misty enter the room.]

MISTY: Yes love!

VICTOR: What do you think of these paintings? Yank found them in his deceased Grand Aunt house, do you think they could be worth something?

[Misty pick up one of the painting and look at it.]

55

MISTY: I like this one, it an excellent painting, look at the lake, the trees, mountains and clouds! It would be just as interesting without the cattle, what do you think? Are they genuine?

VICTOR: I think so, Yank and I are going to Sotheby's for a valuation, I better make a telephone enquiry first.

MISTY: I think they are worth two thousand pounds.

YANK: That would be nice. I see you have the Jerusalem Bible, Haftorah and the Apocrypha, there on the coffee table?

MISTY: Yes, we read them, would you like to borrow one?

YANK: Well If it no trouble.

MISTY: There are four Angels known to us by name, two is in the Bible, and two in the Apocrypha. The Angela Uriel and Raphael are in the Apocrypha. Michael and Gabriel are in the Bible; is the name Gibrel derives from the name Gabriel, it means Angel, also man of God or God is strong.

YANK: I think so, you know us West Indians, we get the spelling wrong.

MISTY: You can borrow the Apocrypha, I think you will find it an interesting read. [She pick up the Apocrypha and hand it to YANK.]

YANK: Thanks.

MISTY: May be you, Elena and Gibrel can join us in church one Sunday.

[Victor, Fez and Yank are in Victor's car, Yank is in the back seat, with his paintings resting next to him, the men are wearing suits.]

FEZ: Don't get me wrong, I'm over the moon about the pregnancy. It's just that we were having terrific sex. I thought it would take about five months, after she stopped taking the pill.

YANK: Aaaa, the side position is the best during the months of pregnancy.

FEZ: Looking forward to it.

VICTOR: About three hundred to five hundred sperm come out in one ejaculation! And it only take one sperm to penetrate the egg.

YANK: Sperm invasion man sperm invasion.

VICTOR: Listen to this, they swim an inch in eight minutes! And a sperm can reach an egg in thirty minutes! Once the sperm get to the uterus, they can live there for four to five days!

FEZ: A warm and cozy place for a holiday.

VICTOR: Once the embryo is one month old, it's the size of a pea! By two months the embryo is called a fetus, it's then about one inch long, and beginning to develop human form. At three months the fetus is about three inch long, just over four months, the fetus heartbeat can be heard; and the mother can start to feel the fetus move.

FEZ: He will know those moves from his father.

VICTOR: Here this, Non-identical twins are developed from two separate eggs! Fertilized by two separate sperm, the sperm and ova have only twenty three chromosome, so when they meet, the single fertilize egg has a full forty six chromosome. A woman's egg contain a single X chromosome! While a man's sperm have both an X or a Y chromosome. If an egg is fertilized by an X chromosome sperm, then the baby is a girl! And if it's fertilized by a Y chromosome sperm, then the baby is a boy.

FEZ: So if the woman's egg is an X, and she is fertilized by an X sperm, it's a girl.

VICTOR: Yes.

YANK: So an X egg and Y sperm mak a boy?

VICTOR: Yes, are you going for natural child birth?

FEZ: I'm going to go to those classes with her, if that's what you mean. I most be there to encourage him out. I shall be saying, you've been in there for nine cozy months, [Loudly.] NOW COME OUT. I shall say to Teresa, I want my boy push. [They laugh.]

VICTOR: It's a great time to get rowdy, just think the world greatest foot-ball player could be in there! [Loudly and spontaneously.]

YANK: Eagles.

VICTOR: Eagles.

FEZ: Eagles. Remind me, what foot-ball team fan cheer name that is.

YANK: Crystal Palace.

VICTOR: It's odd the way women delivered their babies in olden days. The Persian women delivered their babies, by positioning themselves with legs a stride, then resting their knees on a cushion bricks! Using the bricks as a support when pushing! Where as the Iroquois Indians women delivery was to stand, supported by another woman, with a third woman, stoop down to help the baby out! On the other hand, the Madi women of central Africa sat back to back, with clasp arms to support the woman during delivery!

YANK: Men never have nothing to do with delivery in those days?

VICTOR: It would seem not. [Victor is driving up Wigmore Street.]

VICTOR: There's The Wigmore Hall, Cloud goes there, he says the concerts are delightful.

FEZ: Classical music is not my thing.

YANK: Same here, have you been.

VICTOR: Not yet.

[They get out the car and start walking off the stage. LEFT.] [They enter the stage. LEFT. And walk slowly down New Bond Street. They stop and look in the shop window.]

FEZ: If what's his name.

VICTOR: Phillip Pegler.

FEZ: If Phillip Pegler don't say three thousand, I'll will eat my hat, what do you think Yank?

YANK: Well if yu say three thousand, mi wi say give mi five.

VICTOR: Phillip Pegler said he couldn't give me a price, until he see them, but I would say a few thousand more.

YANK: It more than mi would da expect! Mi could do with a new suit.

VICTOR: Suave!

FEZ: Debonair! Likely to cost an arm and a leg.

YANK: A only two suit mi have to mi name.

VICTOR: The price you have to pay! Those suit should be retail besoke.

FEZ: What.

VICTOR: Hand made suits.

YANK: Fi mi suits are off-the-peg, mi know bout suits from wan Tailor, him have a shop on Deptford High Street. Now him could tell yu a thing bout collar stand, collar fall, regency collar, single breasted lapel, waistcoats, and what polish off a good suit is a good tie.

VICTOR: What about the material?

FEZ: It must be cashmere.

[They walk off the stage. RIGHT.] [They enter the stage led by the Security Guard to the

Work of Arts counter. There is a Desk Assistant behind the Work of Arts counter. The Security Guard return to his station. RIGHT.]

    VICTOR: We are here to see Phillip Pegler.
    DESK ASSISTANT: Your name?
    VICTOR: Mister Boaz.
    DESK ASSISTANT: Please stay here I will get him. [He leave and return some second later, followed by Phillip Pegler. LEFT.]
    PHILLIP PEGLER: Mister Boaz.
    VICTOR: We have the painting here.
[Fez and Yank took the news paper off the paintings and hand them to him.]
    PHILLIP PEGLER: First may I establish whose painting they are?
    YANK: Them a fi mi paintings.
[Phillip Pegler look at Yank in astonishment, then proceed to look at the paintings.]
    PHILLIP PEGLER: How long have you owned them?
    VICTOR: How long did your Grand Aunt owned her house?
    YANK: Over forty years.
[Phillip Pegler talk about the paintings with enthusiasm. The men listen to him in awe.]
    PHILLIP PEGLER: Sidney Richard Percy, was an accomplished artist, from eighteen twenty one to eighteen eighty six, a similar painting to this was dated eighteen eighty one; unique, an exquisite glimpse of the most remarkable natural compositions. It reminds the urban dwellers of Scotland most tranquil past. I love it! His powerful depictions of the sky, the lock, the mountains, the trees, and cart in their natural habitat! Look at the quality!
    VICTOR: Where do you think exactly, the scene was painted?
    PHILLIP PEGLER: A number of Sidney Percy's painting were of Scotland, this looks remarkable like Lock Katrine. I am envious of you, having something like this! The painting and its' fascinating originality will attain new heights of brilliance and opulence! It just whispers at you.
[Phillip Pegler put the painting on the desk, and pick up the other painting.]
    PHILLIP PEGLER: Again I am very envious, brilliant colours! And intricate fine composition. Louis Bosworth Hurt, another accomplished artist, from eighteen fifty six to nineteen twenty nine; a similar painting was dated nineteen zero five. I love it! Again look

at the quality! His powerful depiction of highland cattle; these are lavishly painted. The cattle are invariable affiliated with the dramatic scenery, of the harsh weather conditions of the Island of Skye. An increasingly important feature, is the palatial depth of colours in the landscape. Louis Hurt, has produced some of the most exquisite paintings. These are characterized by the powerful depiction of highland cattle, look at the quality!

FEZ: What would you say the paintings are worth?

[Phillip Pegler pick up the first painting.]

PHILLIP PEGLER: This painting, insure it for forty thousand pounds.

[Yank's mouth open in shock. Phillip Pegler put down the painting and pick up the other painting.]

PHILLIP PEGLER: And this painting, insure it for forty five thousand pounds. You have in your possession paintings, which should be insured for eighty-five thousand pounds.

[Victor and Fez look for Yank, he is not standing by them, they look behind them, Yank is on the floor flat on his back. He had passed out in shock. Victor and Fez went to his aid, they slap him on the face, to bring him to consciousness. They stood him to his feet, and brought him to the counter.]

VICTOR: What would you say, he's likely to get for them at Sotheby's auction?

PHILLIP PEGLER: A lot more. An important factor in this market, is the good supply of paintings coming up for sale. Paintings by James McIntosh Patrick for example, often remained in private hands, rather than ending up in a museums. December nineteen ninety seven, was when, one of the five versions of the Danse a L' Arbrde Mai, fetched nineteen million eight hundred and fifteen thousand, at Sotheby's.

[Yank legs went wobbly, Victor and Fez held him up.]

VICTOR: Would you like them to go to auction Yank?

YANK: Yes!

[Phillip Pegler take a form from behind the counter, and a pen from his jacket pocket to write out a written receipt for Yank.]

PHILLIP PEGLER: Your name?

YANK: Ralph Mayer.

Amazing Caring Woman

PHILLIP PEGLER: Your address and telephone number?
[Whilst Yank gives his details, Victor and Fez walk away, Victor search his jacket pocket for his cell phone, to find it not there.]
VICTOR: Fez lend me your cell phone? I would like to talk to Misty.
[Fez hand Victor the phone, and Victor press the numbers into the phone.]
MISTY: Press Office, Royal National Theatre.
VICTOR: Misty get ready for a shock.
MISTY: Hi love.
VICTOR: Yank's paintings are to be insured for eighty-five thousand pounds.
MISTY: Blessed Mary! I can't hardly believe it, eighty-five thousand.
[The garden is wide, with a lawn. It has flowering shrubs, trees and a green broader edge, to the rear of the garden is a cured bench, under a trellis of grape-vine. The play area for the children is a sand pit, and this is to the rear left. In the lawn area of the garden, is round table with chairs. The barbeque is to the right, the food is well presented on a long table, there is another table for the drinks, with a ice barrel full of can lagers. One of the guests is a Chef, and he is behind the barbeque grill cooking, he is wearing a Chef's hat and Chef's tunic. The guest is mingling with glasses of wine or lager, or food in their hands. The guest are Caucasians with two Chinese, two African and one Indian. Sky and her husband Bauer enter, followed by Victor, Fez, Yank, Misty, Teresa and Elena holding Gibrel at her waist and under her arm. LEFT.]
BAUER: It's a smashing day for a barbeque!
VICTOR: It sure is.
BAUER: let me tell you about the guest, to the rear, sitting under the trellis of grape-vine, is Stewart and Gillian, they are Nurses, Jake is our friend and Chef for the day; [Pointing to them.] Cloud Levi Is the Publishing Director for The Glitzey, and Melania his wife is a Dentist. Wen Lin and his wife Kim are Surgeon and Doctor, David Rueben is a Doctor, Tamara Goodman is a Dentist, Joshua Adwoa is a Surgeon, and his wife Shirley is a Doctor; Garrett McGowans is a Doctor and Grainne his wife is the Head Mistress of a Primary School, Thomas Worledge is a Doctor, Frederick Wagstaffe is a Surgeon, Peter Petel is a Doctor, and Helena and Ernest Ferguson are our neighbours.

SKY: Elena let me show you the play area, you can put Gibrel in the sand pit. [They walk to the sand pit, Victor, Fez, Yank and Teresa walk over to the drinks' table, with their bottle of wines. Misty smelling the food suddenly felt sick, she run behind the green broader edge, and began to vomit. Everyone is busy in conversation so they did not notice her.]

HELENA: Surprisingly, the Romans, Saxons, Vikings and Normans were the invading armies.

CLOUD: Oh yes, and those who were to follower, had little choice about coming. Africans were brought to Britain by force, in the seventeen and eighteen centuries, used as slaves or servants. Thousand of people arrived at various times, as refuges from France, Ireland, Russia and other countries. Escaping from persecution or famine. Immigration was of dealing with local shortages, of capital, skills and labour.

KIM: Immigrants have brought skills and qualifications, set up businesses, and created jobs, not only for themselves, but for local people. Many have been willing to do jobs, that have been difficult to fill locally.

TAMARA: In ten sixty six, a small community of French Jews were encouraged by William The First, to bring their capital and financial skills to Britain.

DAVID: Jews were the founders of banking and financial services in Britain. [David, Tamara and Kim walk away.]

JOSHUA: Yes! And from the fourteen century, Flemish and French weavers, German mining engineers, Dutch cannel builders, painters' brewers and brick makers, brought new manufactural skills and techniques at a time, when wool was Britain's only major export. [Ernest walk over and join them.]

GARRETT: Quite! The Irish fled in there thousand, from rural poverty and famine, between the eighteen thirties and eighteen fifties, they helped to build much of the infrastructure of the industrial society in Britain.

[Melania walk over and join them.]

GRAINNE: In deed! Doing work that local people often didn't want. In mines, docks, and building cannals, roads, railways and factories.

JOSHUA: I'll say! British traders and merchants' had made

fortunes, through the trade in the Americas' and West Indies. [Garrett and Grainne walk away.]

ERNEST: Yes! The British Empire owed its success to over two million Indian and Chinese labourer, who worked on plantations, mines, docks, ships and railroads.

MELANIA: Britain was faced with the massive task of reconstruction, after the second world war, and acute labour shortages. British Government encouraged immigration from Ireland and the commonwealth. An over whelming majority of workers were Africans, Asian and Caribbean.

CLOUD: [He knows that physician in ancient times were considered to be gods.] What have we here! Historians or Aesculapian!

HELENA: [Pointing to Ernest.] We are the neighbours.

CLOUD: How about aesthetics, would you like to try some of the food?

WEN: Sure, my taste buds is watering,

JOSHUA: I'm famylous. [Cloud, Wen and Joshua walk over to the food table, and help them-selves with food. Sky is talking to Stewart and Gillian, saw Misty behind the green boarder edge, she walk over to her.]

SKY: Are you? [Misty heaved again.] I will get you some water. [Sky walk over to the drinks table and got her a glass of water, and brought it back to Misty. Here drink this, she drank some water, and walk round from behind the edge, they both walk to the table and sat down.]

SKY: Does Victor Know?

MISTY: I think we will both be sure now!

SKY: [Sky kiss Misty.] So I'm going to be a auntie again, I'm over joyed! Congratulations!

MISTY: Thank you.

SKY: I will go and get Victor. [Sky walk over to Victor at the drinks table, Cloud walk over to Thomas and Frederick, they are having a discussion.]

THOMAS: Aaaa, Cloud.

CLOUD: Hi.

[Frederick accentuated the accent of the Professor and the Doctor.]

FREDERICK: The man had a terrible disease of his guts, and all those clever Doctors and Professor of this and that and the other, took him to pieces, literally! They got no where, near finding out what was wrong with him.

THOMAS: Surly not!

FREDERICK: After about fifteen years he died! At the post-mortem conference, the professor of medicine turned to the family Doctor and said. "Can you tell us something about the home life of this patient"; the family Doctor said, "I think this man is a case of aesthematology".

THOMAS: You surprise me!

FREDERICK: It started when his father died, then got worse when his adopted daughter made what he regarded as an unsatisfactory marriage; and the final relapse followed by his death. This occurred when he was sacked from his job, he'd put in many years of hard work, and he was sacked without any kind of adequate recompense made to him.

CLOUD: It's not surprising, what an alethiology.

FREDERICK: The Professor of medicine said, yes thank you very much, but I don't think we can take psychological facts into account here. They took absolutely no notice of that man! Because Doctors don't have a frame work of reference, to enable them to translate things like anger or sadness into diseases. [They laugh.]

[Victor walk over to Misty and sat at the table. He could see the beaming look on her face, he knew what the news was going to be, however he wanted her to say it.]

MISTY: I'm pregnant!

VICTOR: [He hug her and kiss her.] Are you sure?

MISTY: As sure as I can be.

VICTOR: It's the best news every my love. [They kiss.]

MISTY: I love you.

VICTOR: I love you infinitely.

MISTY: Our blessing and praises are to God.

VICTOR: Yes. What about our holiday!

MISTY: It will be ok, vomiting, hopefully should not last for long. Jokingly, I would like to follow my family tradition, and call our children names like lightening, rain or thunder. [They laugh.]

[Yank is wandering around the garden, he walk past Stewart and Gillian sitting under the trellis of grape-vine.]

GILLIAN: You gave me thrush.

STEWART: No I did not.

GILLIAN: Yes you did.

[Yank did not here their conversation correctly, he is now walking to Elena, who is listening to the conversation between Fez, Thomas, Shirley and Joshua.]

THOMAS: Habituate to the foreign tissues of the epidermis, treatment is to render proof, against the prejudicial influence of a foreign existence.

[Yank pulled Elena away, he look toward the trellis, then to Elena and whisper.]

YANK: You see that man over there, him trashed a woman!

ELENA: Mi no understand a word they say! [Yank and Elena walk to the drink table.]

FEZ: No! My family are from Africa.

SHIRLEY: Forgive the cliché, when someone mention Africa, I often think of black people, what country are you from?

FEZ: My ancestors started out in Senegal, then they moved to Nigeria, then to Morocco.

JOSHUA: [He shake Fez hand.] It's a pleasure to meet a man who's ancestors were Senegalese, I'm from Petit Cote, it's south from Daker.

FEZ: I was actually born here, my ancestors are from Saint Louis.

SHIRLEY: Aaaa yes! It's in the north, have you been there?

FEZ: No, but I would like to go there one day.

JOSHUA: Senegal was one of the first part of west Africa, to be inhabited by humans, do you know, they found human remains there dating back to thirteen thousand BC!

FEZ: No!

THOMAS: In fact the Europeans arrived there in fourteen forty four, they were the medieval Europeans, the Portuguese traders landed there, of course they scoured the coast in search of slaves. It was the French who secured the country in the late sixteen hundreds.

JOSHUA: Yes yes, in fact the Ghana Empire flourished between the eight and eleventh centuries. As the Ghana Empire grip weakened Islamic invaders from Morocco reach Senegal.

[Thomas walk away.]

FEZ: It make sense! To know why I have relatives in Morocco, and they had started out in Senegal.

JOSHUA: It's funny you should mention it, because a famous black Politician named Leopold Senghor, who couldn't speak Wolof, the native language, and was a Catholic in an over whelming Muslim

country, married a white French woman.
[Teresa walk over to them.]

    FEZ: [Putting his arm around Teresa.] My wife Teresa family is from Saint Lucia.

    SHIRLEY: Hi.

    JOSHUA: Hi.

    TERESA: Hi.

    JOSHUA: You should visit Senegal, there is an impressive bird sanctuary in Djoudi National Park. Almost three hundred species of birds have been recorded there.

    TERESA: How magnificent! It's a part of the world we would like to visit one day.

    JOSHUA: How about a drink?

[Joshua, Shirley, Fez and Teresa walk over to the drink table.] [Sky is talking to Jake they are on the lawn away from the grill.]

    SKY: You have excelled your-self as usual, they are enjoying your delights.

    JAKE: [He speaks with a light-hearted smile.] I should think so, to think of the time, and my skills in preparing such a feast.

    SKY: Don't leave my guests out of your praises, some have brought a dish remember.

    JAKE: Well said, it's a great barbeque. [They knock their glasses together, and sip their wine.]

[Bauer and Frederick walk over to Thomas and Shirley, Frederick is very drunk. He put his arm around Bauer. Sky walk over to them, just in time to here what Frederick said.]

    FREDERICK: You know Thomas, Bauer is a kalokagathia.

    BAUER: Thank you.

    SKY: [She is surprise by the compliment, because it is from an elderly and an highly accomplished Doctor.] So my husband is the goodness of character! [SKY kiss Bauer.]

[Peter is walking near by, he took a small box from his pocket and open it, then took out a pill and put it in his mouth, they look at him.]

    PETER: [He is referring to the box of pill.] A pilole you know.

    SHIRLEY: What's your problem?

    PETER: Hay fever, even Doctors are affected by the crisis of

health. [Loud noise come from children playing in the sand pit.] Who made that brayt! [The other look in the children direction.]
[Elena take Gibrel out of the sand pit, and hold him at her waist and under her arm. Thomas walk over to them.]

    GIBREL: Look what I found.

[Elena gently open his hand Thomas look in his hand.]

    THOMAS: What we have here! Aaaa gryllus.

    ELENA: No! It's a grasshopper. [Elena put Gibrel back in the sand pit.]

[Thomas return to them.]

    SHIRLEY: Where are you from Bauer?

    BAUER: I'm from Saint Croix, one of the British Virgin Islands.

    SHIRLEY: The Caribbean!

    BAUER: As you can see I'm mixed race, the Island is a mixture of French, African and Puerto Ricans.

    THOMAS: I believe the original name for the Island was Santa Cruz.

[Victor, Misty, Fez, Teresa, Yank and Elena are standing together, kissing Misty hugging her and laughing. Bauer and Sky is standing a distance away from their guest, looking at them. Bauer's arm is around Sky's shoulder.]

    BAUER: They are having a good time!

    SKY: Lots of good news over there, Misty is pregnant.

    BAUER: Superb!

    SKY: Teresa is also pregnant!

    BAUER: Wanderfull!

[Sky reiterated some of Elena's realistic desires.]

    SKY: Elena told me Yank came into money! They are looking for a house on, Lee Park road, and they are going into business with Fez. Elena is looking for a bigger hair dress shop; she wants to start driving lessons, and in a years-time, they are going to try for their second baby.

    BAUER: Some people have all the luck.

CURTAIN

Glossary

Assam	Known brand of tea
Alcorza	A kind of sweet meat
Allah	Arabic means God
Arawak Indians	Original people in Jamaica
Albert Finney	British Actor
Anthony Newley	British Actor
Alai Kun Salam	Upon you peace
Aesculapian	An ancient healing god
Aesthetics	The doctrine of taste
Aesthematology	A branch of physiology treating the senses
Alethiology	The doctrine of truth and error in logic
Brook Bond PG tips	Known brand of tea
Beef patties	Jamaican patties made with pastry
Brandy	Genuine name of a horse
Bout	Patois for about
Between the sheets	Name of a cocktail
Blue lagoon	Name of a cocktail
Byron's verse	So we'll go no more a-rowing
Byron's verse	Sonnet of George the fourth
BBC	British Broadcasting Corporation
Babby Kristin	Whitney Houston's daughter.
British Empire	Historical fact
Brayt	A loud yell
Cantering	A gallop on a horse
Calvados	Name of a cocktail
Classic	Name of a cocktail
Crystal Palace	A town in London
Calabash Day Centre	Day centre for the elderly black pensioners
Chippendale	Expensive antique furniture
Cow and Chicken	Cartoon characters
Cuscus	Moroccan dish

Chey-bon-jen	Senegalese National dish
Custard apple	Jamaican fruit
Callaloo	Jamaican vegetable, similar to spinach
Cashmere	Known fabric
Di	Patois for the, they or did
Dulwich	A town in London
Dem no	Patois for they don't
Delivery [babies]	Our bodies ourselves, Jill Rakusen
Deptford	A town in London
Djoudi National Park	In Senegal
Early Grey	Known brand of tea
Euphoria	Feeling of happiness
Ecstasy	Intense delight
Ebony	African American Magazine
Eagles	Crystal Palace foot-ball fans cheer name
Face muscles	Fact. Dorling Kindersley
Freud Sigmund	Author and psycho-analysis
Fi	Patios for your, for, our, and should
Fatty boom boom	Old Reggae song
Foyer	Reception area in the theatre
Felicity Kendal	British Actress
Flemish/ French	Historical fact
Famylous	Desperately hungry
Guavas	Tropical fruit
Greenwich	A town in London
Gabrielle Jourdon	Theatre Actress
Gwaan	Patios for going on
Gryllus	Scientific name for grasshopper
Hair	Fact, Dorling Kindersley

Haftorah	Hebrew bible
Henry Goodman	Theatre Actor
Harnimans Museum	Situated in Forest hill, London
Holy Quran	From the Holy Quran
Hilton Hotel	Central London
Haf	Patios for have
Hidden Treasure	Base on Matthew 13:44, from Christ's object, Lessons growing up in Christ, by Better living Publications
If a child	The Strong Family Bible Study Guide, By Charles R. Swindoll
International whaling	Fact, News Paper article
Immigrants	Historical fact
Irish fled	Historical fact
Jasmine	Known brand of tea
Jung	Author and Psycho-analysis
James Bond	Name of a cocktail
Ja	Rastafarian name for God
June plums	Jamaican fruit
Joanna's	Restaurant in Crystal Palace
Jerk chicken	Jamaican, spice, herbs and scotch bonnet peppers
John Osborne	Play writer
Jerry Springer	American Talk Show Host
Jan Mostaert	Sunday Times Review
Jews/ Banking	Historical fact
Knife and forks	Historical fact, from the British Museum
Kiss mi neck	Jamaican expression of surprise
King Mutebi	King of Uganda
Kalokugathia	Goodness of character
Lady Grey	Known brand of tea
Le Piat D'or	Name of a wine

Lord	Stands for a divine name, it means not by a Mighty hand.
Linford Christie	British sport personality Negro.
Lager	Light colour beer.
Louise B. Hurt	Artist 1856 to 1929.
Lee Park Road	A road in London S.E.3
Mi	Patios for I
Morocco mole	Cartoon character
Mangoes	Tropical fruit
Mak	Patios for make
Mariah Carey	American Singer/Actress
Mash up	Patios for broken up
Maga	Patios for slim or slender
Mackintosh	Expensive antique furniture
Off-the-peg	Factory made suits
Poke	Patios for pout
Prawns	Shimps
Proverbs Chapter 22	The Jerusalem Bible
Picky	Patios for child/children
Peacock	Name of a clothes shop
Paul Boateng	British Home Office Minister, Negro
Pilole.	A small container of pills
Queen Sylvia	Queen of Uganda, Negro
Rasta	Rastafarian unorthodox religion
Riesner	Expensive antique furniture
Rusty Lee	British cook Presenter, Negro
Retail Besoke	Handmade suits
Royal National Theatre	Situated in Central London
Stevie Wander	American Singer/Song writer

Sugar dumpling	Round fried sugar dough, term of endearment
Sweet bread	Delicacy sheep testicle
Speel	Untruth
Screaming orgasm	Name of a cocktail
Slow comfortable screw	Name of a cocktail
Secret Squirrel	Cartoon character
Saint Dunstans college	Private Secondary Boys School
Soave	Name of a wine
Star apples	Jamaican fruit
Sweet cup	Jamaican fruit
Serviettes	Napkins
Sa	Patios for say
Scoop	Journalist story
Squeeze with knees	Instructions for horses
Scandinavian	Historical fact
Shakespeare	Author/ Play writer Classic
Salam alai kun	Peace be upon you
Saint Thomas Hospital	Situated in Central London
Settee	A couch
Stoosh	Upper class / high tone
Sotheby's	Auctioneers Central London
Sidney R. Percy	Artist 1821 to 1886
Senegal	Historical fact
Saint Croix	Historical fact
The Glitzey	Fictional name
Trot	Running action of a horse
Three rivers	Name of a cocktail
Tak	Patios for take
Tom Courtney	British Actor
The man	True story, Library book
Thrush	Infection of the vagina
Trashed	To hit repeatedly
Uno	Patios for you all

Vodka	Genuine name of a horse
Valpolicella	Name of a wine
Whisky	Genuine name of a horse
Whatever we	Adapted from the Holy Quran
White Germans	Historical fact, Jamaican Embassy
Whitney Houston	American pop star/ movie star, The Voice News paper
Wi	Patios for we
Wa	Patios for what
Wigmore Hall	Classical Music concert hall, Central London
Ye	Patios for yes
Yu	Patios for you
Ya	Patios for here
Yai	Patios for eye
Y and X chromosome	Doctor Miriam Stoppard, Conception, Pregnancy and Birth

www.ingramcontent.com/pod-product-compliance
Lightning Source LLC
LaVergne TN
LVHW021120080426
835510LV00012B/1775